Who Controls Our Schools?

The common school was to include children from all classes, sects, and ethnic groups. The common school crusaders (largely British-American in ethnic origin, middle class in economic status, and evangelistically Protestant in religious orientation) believed that a common school, controlled and financed largely by local trustees and public taxation was essential to the millennial destiny of a righteous republic.

WHO CONTROLS OUR SCHOOLS?

AMERICAN VALUES IN CONFLICT

MICHAEL W. KIRST

W.H. Freeman and Company
New York

This book was published originally as a part of *The Portable Stanford*, a series of books published by the Stanford Alumni Association, Stanford, California.

Library of Congress Cataloging in Publication Data

Kirst, Michael W.
    Who controls our schools.

    Bibliography: p.
    Includes index.
    1. Education—United States—Aims and objectives.
    2. Curriculum planning—United States. I. Title.
LA217.K57 1985 4   370'.973   84-25881
ISBN 0-7167-1719-0
ISBN 0-7167-1720-4 (pbk.)

Printed in the United States of America

9 8 7 6 5 4 3 2 1 ML 1 0 8 9 8 7 6 5 4 3

CONTENTS

FOREWORD

Before the galleys of Michael Kirst's new book reached me, I prepared some questions stimulated by its title. When I read it, I
found that he had addressed them all. His very first words, "As
president of the California State Board of Education ..." indicate his
angle of vision. Like the classic Chinese painter, he occupies a place
above the earth yet below the mountaintop. From this perspective,
which he maintains consistently throughout the book, he is able to
focus on the larger issues without neglecting the gritty realities.

The 1980s are and will surely continue to be the decade of the states
in the affairs of the schools. As a major state official and as a scholar,
Professor Kirst can see, to use his words, that "the pendulum swings
back and forth, but rarely all the way back." He does not paint a
peaceful landscape; there are storm clouds, and the people on the
ground are scurrying about, occasionally in circles. He is well aware
of the competing objectives of the numerous groups interested in the
schools, and he does not shy away from the troubles caused when
one special interest pushes the schools out of balance.

The chapter entitled "Renewing the Teaching Profession" is the most
concise and devastating discussion I have read on this important
subject. And his chapter on textbooks—which have far more to do
with what goes on in the classroom than one likes to admit—should
be required reading. Addressing the question, "How Well Do Our
Schools Perform?" (Chapter 5), Professor Kirst writes, and shows to
this reader's satisfaction, that "when we set clear goals and pursue
them—with patience—we can improve our schools' performance." He
shows that he can lead the way.

Francis Keppel

ACKNOWLEDGMENTS

Several of the major ideas in this volume were refined in a course for Stanford undergraduates jointly taught with David Tyack. We both benefited from the comments and reactions of our students.

Who Controls Our Schools? is the product of an intense collaborative effort. My editor, JoAn Johnstone, helped to develop in a fundamental way its concept and text. An impeccably thorough editor, she read my earlier books and articles and wove together pertinent material to enhance this book. Miriam Miller, editor of The Portable Stanford series, helped to develop the outline and identify the themes and gave every chapter its final polish. Laura Ackerman-Shaw, production manager of The Portable Stanford, searched out photographs and cartoons, redesigned tables and figures, and shepherded the book through all its phases from manuscript to bound book. Stephanie Sandberg typed the manuscript with care and intelligence. I hope this will not be the last time we all produce a book together.

The discussion of nineteenth-century education, the rise of vocational education, and the post-World War II period draws heavily on Professor Tyack's article, "The High School as a Social Service Agency: Historical Perspectives on Current Policy Issues," *Educational Evaluation and Policy Analysis* (September-October, 1979): 45-57. I have also used revised versions of studies I have published elsewhere, alone or in collaboration with others: "Educational Reform: Retrospect and Prospect," *Teachers College Record* 81 (Spring 1980): 253-69, prepared under the auspices of the National Institute of Education and jointly authored with David B. Tyack and Elisabeth Hansot. *Schools in Conflict* (Berkeley: McCutchan, 1982) with Frederick M. Wirt. *State School Fi-*

nance Alternatives (Eugene: University of Oregon, 1975) with Larry Pierce, Walter Garms, and James Guthrie. "Choosing Textbooks," *American Educator* (Summer 1984). "The Changing Politics of Education: Actions and Strategies," in Edith Mosher, ed., *The Changing Politics of Education: Prospects for the 1980s* (Berkeley: McCutchan, 1978). "The Shifting Balance in State/Local Control," *Phi Delta Kappan* (November, 1984).

PREFACE

Once again we are being alerted to a "crisis in our schools." Political leaders, national commissions, and the media have pointed with alarm to declining student achievement, a warning sign, they say, of a pervasive mediocrity that threatens our ability to compete successfully in international markets. In September 1984, ABC television devoted three hours of prime time to a program exploring a subject once more familiar to noncommercial television—the deterioration of our schools.

This book will attempt to place in historical perspective the current concern with how well our schools perform their function. Americans have frequently given intense scrutiny to education, asking whether the policies governing the schools are designed to promote the best in youth behavior and achievement. To one familiar with earlier eras in education, the current crisis has familiar overtones.

But the aim here is to move beyond the history of education to an understanding of today's education policies. Often the media give the impression that a distant group, insulated from politics and impervious to public concern, formulates the policies that control education. In reality, the groups and "publics" that govern education are many and diverse. Americans have always believed that education policy is too important to leave to educators. Now, as in the past, an aroused citizenry can powerfully influence school policy. But education policy is a complex subject. To be effective in shaping policy requires a sophisticated understanding of the history of education and of current patterns of control. Without such an understanding, today's aroused citizens may become frustrated citizens, unprepared for the complexities they must face. They should be aware, for example, that the current movement for higher academic standards and required courses runs directly opposite to the public pressure exerted not so long ago (1968-72) for student options and curricular diversification. In both eras, the schools responded and changed directions.

This book reflects the author's experience in government, in private consulting, and in academic research. Each of the 44 faculty members of Stanford's School of Education could write an interesting and authoritative volume on his or her special field. I have not attempted to cover many fascinating subjects, such as how children learn, or what is the best way to teach reading, or how computers can be used effectively in the classroom. But I have tried to provide an overview of the key issues facing education as an American institution and by addressing broad areas—among these, curricular priorities, finance, governance, and the teaching profession—a framework into which the reader can fit other or more specialized issues.

Michael W. Kirst

Stanford University
December 1984

CHAPTER

IS SOMETHING WRONG WITH OUR SCHOOLS?

As president of the California State Board of Education in 1980, I found myself a magnet for the expression of opinions on American public schools. The mere mention of my state position at any gathering would almost invariably prompt criticism from a surprising variety of perspectives. Some people complained about poor college preparation; others bemoaned their children's lack of self-confidence; still others criticized the level of vocational skill development or the quality of high school music and basketball. And these complaints were voiced by residents of California, a state where 57 percent of the high school graduates went on to college and the technology-based economy was booming!

People I met also questioned me about the various measures of school performance reported—superficially—in the newspapers. One woman wanted to know why the scores of California students on the Scholastic Aptitude Test (SAT) were lower than those in Arkansas and why our school system was not as good as Arkansas's. I explained that only 5 percent of Arkansas's high school seniors take the SAT (most of them applicants to selective out-of-state institutions), while in California, 35 percent of the high school seniors take the SAT because all four-year public universities in the state—and these are the schools they aspire to—require it. The newspaper was comparing two vastly different student populations. Beyond that distortion, there are so many goals for education that a single statistic on college aptitude is a ludicrous oversimplification of academic performance, and therefore of the value of education.

"I'm not an underachiever. You're an overexpecter." Is something wrong with our schools?

My business friends frequently complained that the school system was controlled by educators and "low quality local school board members." It was clear that they were under the impression that the state government did not have much say about education, when, in fact, California's state education code comprises five volumes so thick they would sprain the back of almost any adult who tried to lift them.

These same critics, however, did not hesitate to lobby me for more state regulation to meet their special concerns. One woman wanted a state graduation requirement for art. (Art programs had been drastically curtailed in 1979 after Proposition 13 cut California's property tax rate in half.) Another wanted a study of the dangers of nuclear war added to the curriculum in social studies. Still another asked me to help eliminate bilingual education, so that California would not "end up like French-speaking Quebec."

Even though I was on the state board of education from 1975 to 1981, I was—and again, few people seemed aware of the facts—just one of hundreds of state policymakers, not to mention the 7,000 locally elected school board members in California who oversee 220,000 teachers and $12 billion worth of expenditures. (To arrive at an approximation of the national figures, just multiply all these numbers by ten.) During my six years on the state board, we managed to please some of the school constituencies some of the time; but because there were so many special interest groups, most were unhappy more often than not. They all wanted "higher priority" for their particular needs—more school time or money and "more input" into school policy making. Parents of gifted children complained of inadequate funds. Parents of autistic children noted that blind and deaf children had more favorable pupil/teacher ratios, despite their "milder handicaps."

As I attempted to assess these discontents, I was forced to pose two questions: Is something wrong with our schools? and By what criteria shall we determine the answer? I concluded that the answer lay in large part in the insistence of the American public that the schools be and do everything for everyone. Moreover, the American people, following a process deeply rooted in the history of our nation, are politically organized to achieve their all-embracing goal. The result is an ongoing conflict for control of the school curriculum. Private schools can focus on college preparation or cosmetology, but the public school is a one-stop shopping center. The public high school is expected to include a store to cater to every consumer taste from sewing to conversational German. As new social problems generate new needs, these are dealt with by merely adding another unit to the curriculum of the secondary or the elementary school. The inevitable, and undesirable, result is the third-grade teacher who must cover English, math, science, social studies, music, art, morality, good manners, and a myriad of state requirements like the importance of kindness to animals and the attributes of free enterprise.

If we look at the recent reports on education and at other warning signs, we may conclude that only our secondary schools are in difficulty. It is in the secondary schools that test scores have declined, rates of graduation decreased, and problems of discipline grown. We can measure a decline in the number of courses taken in higher-level mathematics, social studies, and foreign languages; the curriculum appears fractured and fragmented. But it is the elementary school that provides the essential foundation for the high school. Consequently, this volume will examine all levels of public school education.

My purpose is to do more than analyze the shortcomings of education policy in the United States. Our educational system is a mixture of successes and performance problems, viewed through a cloud of unrealistic expectations. In the chapters to follow I will offer some remedies for the problems—where real problems exist. My general argument, however, is that the American people—who ultimately con-

Jacob Riis, "Saluting the Flag at the Mott Street Industrial School" (1889-90). A major rationale for establishing common schools was to transmit a common culture to a nation of immigrants. Nine million entered in the peak decade of 1900-1910.

Winslow Homer, *The Country School* (1871). Under the guidance of a composed young woman, pupils grouped by age recite or study. Though some share books, in this idealized one-room school children achieve literacy in an atmosphere of simplicity, harmony, and order. In 1860, 80 percent of Americans lived in rural areas.

trol the system—must make a difficult choice: Either surrender some of the numerous objectives we now hold for the schools, or give the public schools a longer school year and much greater resources. Right now we are trying to have it both ways. Schools must do all we ask of them in a year of only 175 days and do it with a low-paid staff whose profession is neither efficiently organized nor held in high esteem.

I hope this book will enable the reader to place the weekly newspaper headlines about education in some broader context. Education policy will always generate controversy and criticism, but it is important to understand the root causes and history of current events. Moreover, I hope that the reader will be able to perceive—realistically—some fruitful direction and strategic political coalition for improving education. I will not provide a detailed blueprint but will focus on changes in direction that our future policies should follow.

CHAPTER

CYCLES OF REFORM— CRISES IN EDUCATION

Shaken by reports that Japanese children were doing much better academically than American children, the California State Board of Education in the early 1980s suddenly changed its agenda. We cut short our formerly intensive discussions of high school dropouts, disadvantaged minorities, and the lower third of the achievement band to focus on the alleged crisis of decline in academic standards. At about the same time, a retired Stanford colleague reported that he was being deluged with invitations to speak on math, science, and technical education—he had not been in such demand since Sputnik went up in 1957. When I asked him why he was suddenly so popular, he replied that the cycle had come around again; he was being asked to speak about the same subject his 1957-59 speeches had addressed— the need to give higher priority to math and science. I resolved to save my old speeches on dropouts and the disadvantaged until the early 1990s, when *that* cycle comes around again. The metaphor of education policy as a bandwagon in search of recurrent crises seems apt.

Cycles of Reform and Multiple Constituencies

Why do we have these cycles? If Americans want their schools to do almost everything and the schools lack the instructional time and the financial resources to do all of it well, then the cycles reflect the correction period when power shifts. The former political "outs" are becoming the political "ins," and one set of priorities is replaced by another. Each cycle gives way to a new cycle because of shocks external to the schools, shocks triggered by social and economic events: im-

TABLE 2-1

High School Graduates, 1870–1970

Year	Total Number (in thousands)	Percentage of 17-Year-Olds	Male (in thousands)	Female (in thousands)
1970	2,906	75.6%	1,439	1,467
1965	2,665	76.3	1,314	1,351
1960	1,864	63.4	898	966
1950	1,200	57.4	571	629
1940	1,221	49.0	579	643
1935	965	41.1	459	506
1930	667	28.8	300	367
1925	528	24.4	230	298
1920	311	16.3	124	188
1915	240	12.8	99	140
1910	156	8.6	64	93
1905	119	7.2	47	72
1900	95	6.3	38	57
1890	44	3.5	19	25
1880	24	2.5	11	13
1870	16	2.0	7	9

Source: Bureau of the Census, 1970 Census (Washington, D.C.: U.S. Government Printing Office, 1970).

About 85 percent of American youth attend high school, and about 75 percent of them are graduated from high school. As recently as 1940, fewer than 50 percent completed high school. In most other Western nations, students are diverted into vocational and technical programs at age 14 or 15, and only 15 to 30 percent are graduated from a secondary school.

migration at the beginning of this century; economic depression in the 1930s; Sputnik in 1957; civil rights in the 1960s; the Vietnam War in the 1970s; and the recession of the early 1980s, as our manufacturing industries lost their competitive advantage over foreign competitors.

Public schools are not the only institutions enmeshed in these cycles of political pressure and bargaining. Stanford and other universities dropped foreign language and history of Western civilization requirements in the 1970s only to restore them in the 1980s. Other institutions of higher education have gone through abrupt changes in their programs and policies only to turn around a decade or a generation later with a new departure that looks much like an older consensus. So the cycles run through all levels of American education, as multiple constituencies create multiple objectives.

In elementary and secondary education, these constituencies built up over the many years of institutional expansion that occurred as the United States increased its high school retention rate from 10 percent to 85 percent (see Table 2-1). An increasingly diverse population of students required more and more varied programs to serve their needs. Academic objectives were supplemented, for instance, by new goals like "worthy use of home and leisure."

A glance at the newspapers over the past few decades leaves one with the impression that education policy is a flotilla of sailboats tacking into strong, shifting winds. Despite the changes that have occurred at the level of policy, this metaphor does not fit the reality of schools as they operate from day to day in American communities. In fact, the schools accrete changes while holding to many basic traditions. A visit to any classroom would reveal that the teaching approach has not changed appreciably over the past 50 years. Teachers, for the most part, still talk from a position in front of the room to children sitting in rows. No new technology has intruded behind the classroom door to be put to regular use since the blackboard. Similarly, structural additions and reorganizations keep increasing the school's functions and objectives, but the school year still ends in June, anachronistically reflecting the agricultural calendar of the nineteenth century. All this suggests that education policy is more like a gigantic oil tanker rolling slightly this way and that in a strong sea.

When cycles of education policy leave lasting deposits as structural accretions, such as vocational education and driver training, they do so for a political reason: Each of the lasting additions is sustained by an organized constituency. School lunch is another. As president of the state board of education at a time when economy was a key value, I advocated using private caterers for school lunch on a competitive bid basis. That idea was squelched by the national organization of school lunch supervisors, a group harkening back to an earlier period when social service was a leading concern.

The schools can please some of these constituencies for a while, but as the external context becomes favorable to their interests, the "low priority" groups mobilize and priorities are shifted again. Thus science educators must seize the opportunity offered by dramatic events like Sputnik, just as advocates of compensatory education seized upon the War on Poverty in 1964. These cycles cannot, however, overcome fundamental alterations in the fabric of American society. Certainly, many of the educational gains that grew out of the civil rights movement of the 1960s will endure. And no matter what the short-term priorities dictate, over the long run the growing number of working women with school-age children will compel more public spending

". . . and the reason we have summer vacation is so you can go home to help with the crops."

for child care. The pendulum swings back and forth, but rarely all the way back.

Like other social institutions in the United States, public schools are judged by current expectations. No credit is given by clients or critics for yesterday's victories. Moreover, new problems arise from the solutions to earlier problems. Clearly, both the dramatic increase in the number of students who go on to a college education and the decline in dropouts are laudable. But the addition of these pupils has resulted in a broader menu of high school courses, which in turn has sparked criticisms of a smorgasbord curriculum that causes a "rising tide of mediocrity." Students may have heard of Plato, Dickens, or Tolstoy, but they know nothing of their works—they "didn't take that course."

Other nations do not hold so many expectations for their schools. In West Germany, the schools leave extracurricular activities to other local agencies. Unlike Americans, Germans do not want their schools to retain the maximum number of youth aged 15 to 17; those not bound for college are sorted out of the system by age 14. In the United

States, on the other hand, every teen-age dropout is seen as a failure of the school system. The Japanese do not attempt vocational education or offer courses on homemaking and crafts. No wonder these nations can do better for the average student on many conventional academic tasks. And it is little consolation that no nation can equal our high-school football teams or cheerleading squads. Or consider this: One Texas pupil missed 30 days of school in 1983 because he was busy exhibiting his prize chicken at agricultural competitions! But at the same time, no nation can equal the United States in the percentage of students who go on to academic colleges or universities.

The American people control the system of education in the United States, and they get what they want. They want a great deal and are organized to get it. They elect one hundred thousand local school board members and thousands of state legislators. State legislatures now provide over 50 cents of the education dollar and exert considerable influence over local education policy. Consequently, state capitals abound with organized pressure groups for gifted children, educational television, and so on. But this citizen involvement is the essence of American democracy and of a political tradition that regards education as too important to be left solely to professional educators. Given the importance of education to their children's future, parent concern and lobbying are understandable.

There was a time when the local superintendent of instruction held a preeminent position in setting an agenda and shaping decisions. Now, the local superintendent and administrative staff have become mostly reactive, as they try to juggle diverse and changing coalitions formed around different issues and operating across different levels of government. Part of the legacy of prior eras has been a tremendous growth in the specialized functions of the school, requiring additions to staff that include administrative specialists in vocational education, driver's education, nutrition, health, remedial reading, and more. These program specialists, paid by federal or state funds directed by law toward special categories of students (handicapped, below poverty level, and so on) have been insulated from the superintendent's influence by the requirements of state and federal government. Their allegiance is often primarily to the higher levels of educational governance, rather than to the local community. As a result, the influence of the superintendent and local school board has been diluted.

I see nothing happening to reverse this trend in the 1980s. Squeezed from the top by the growing influence of federal government, state government, and the courts, superintendents and local boards have found their discretion to make decisions squeezed from the bottom by the growth of local collective bargaining contracts reinforced by national teachers' organizations. Moreover, the influence of special interest groups and professional "reformers" has expanded.

During the 1960s special interest groups, often resulting from nationwide social movements, penetrated the local system, introducing such topics as civil rights, women's roles, students' rights, ethnic self-determination, and bilingual education, and agitating for various changes in the standard operating procedures of the local schools. For example, in many areas students can no longer be expelled without "due process," meaning lengthy hearings with carefully defined procedures. Traditional parent groups, such as the PTA and the American Association of University Women, that once provided support for local school authorities, have become less influential in policy decision making.

Beleaguered local policymakers found by the end of the 1970s that their already constricted area of discretion was growing smaller still—again owing to outside forces, this time primarily economic and demographic. The declining population of students and a spreading resistance to increases in school taxes further constrained local initiatives and options. The early 1980s have brought a period of disillusionment with professionals in general and educators in particular. Distrust has grown as more claimants at the local level squabble over a limited resource base of support for the public schools.

The social movements of the last century were devoted to building up new institutions like the public schools. Since the 1960s, many social movements have been questioning the legitimacy of these public institutions with a view to making them more responsive to forces outside the local administrative structure. The litany of the newspapers cites violence, vandalism, and declining test scores as representing the state of public education and further encourages federal or state intervention to "shape up" the local school policymakers. All of these political forces are causing the process of school decision making to fragment in such a way that local citizens cannot control local school policy. Citizens go to the local school board and superintendent expecting redress of their complaints, only to find that the decision-

making power is not there. The impression grows that no one is in charge of public education.

As the schools suffer increasingly from shock and overload, the key issue becomes: How much change and agitation can an institution bear while continuing to respond to its local clients and voters?

All of this does not mean that local authorities are helpless. Rather, it means they cannot control their agenda or structure the outcome of decisions as they could in the past. The local school superintendent must now deal with shifting and ephemeral coalitions at various governmental levels, coalitions that provide marginal advantages for a brief period.

It is simplistic to describe this changing governance as "centralization." There is no single central control point, but rather a fragmented collection of policymakers beyond the local school board: Congress, state legislatures, and the courts; outside interests such as the Educational Testing Service, the Ford Foundation, the Council for Basic Education, or the Council for Exceptional Children; local internal interests, such as the vocational education coordinators; and local external agencies, such as the police and the health services. All of these have an impact upon education policy.

The shift of authority to higher levels of government has not in all instances resulted in a commensurate loss of local influence. Organized parents of handicapped and bilingual students have considerably more impact on local school boards than they did 25 years ago. Indeed, as the interested parties who demand a role in making education policy increase in number, discretion at the school level may also increase. One outside force can be played off against another. In sum, governance of education is becoming more complex. Concepts such as bureaucratization and centralization imply clear hierarchies of control that do not exist.

A political system with everybody and nobody in charge, pulled in different directions, will continue to trigger recurrent cycles of "crisis," as the too numerous goals of the system—goals that cannot be reached simultaneously—create public discontent with the performance of the public schools. A new coalition of individuals and organizations is needed to refocus educational policy and overcome the current fragmented structure of control.

Cycles of Reform and the Media

By the end of 1985, over 20 national commissions will report on the ills of secondary schools, often in rhetoric that is accusatory and strident. One of ten major reports on education filed in 1983, the report of the National Committee on Excellence in Education, chaired by David Gardner, president of the University of California, set the tone, in metaphors of war and surrender.

> If an unfriendly power had attempted to impose on America the mediocre educational performance that exists today, we might well have viewed it as an act of war. . . . We . . . have . . . squandered the gains in student achievement made in the wake of the Sputnik challenge. . . . We have, in effect, been committing an act of unthinking, unilateral educational disarmament.

Entitled "A Nation at Risk: The Imperative for Educational Reform," the report warns that "a rising tide of mediocrity" threatens our schools, the economy, and the nation. This and other reports have brought nationwide concern for education to the center stage of national and state debates.[1]

Between 1982 and 1984, over 200 high-level state commissions were formed to improve public education. Florida and Mississippi have held special sessions of their legislatures to consider educational reform. The governor of Tennessee, Lamar Alexander, asked his state to do the same: "The quality of the legislation will be best if the legislature gives education all of its attention until it has finished the job." In August 1983, South Carolina's governor, Richard Riley, announced a major program "to raise our public schools from the bottom of the list." In June 1984, the South Carolina state legislature voted a one-cent increase in the state sales tax to fund the program proposed. The same month, the Texas legislature passed the biggest tax increase in that state's history to improve education. In California, Governor George Deukmejian put funding for educational improvement at the top of his budget, explaining, "It has been said that excellence can't be bought, but it must be paid for. Parents and taxpayers are willing to pay for improvements in their children's education—but only if significant reforms are achieved and if we have solid results. We will be looking to the education community to deliver as promised."[2]

These years in the 1980s are for education what the early 1970s were for environmental issues. Many will recall the intense interest in the environment after Earth Day in 1972. Only a few years later, Congress voted extensive regulations promoting cleaner air and water. Similarly, in the 1960s, sit-ins and confrontations between demonstrators and police dramatized the passionate involvement of many Americans in the struggle for civil rights, and the urban riots following the assassination of Dr. Martin Luther King, Jr. raised the issues of big-city problems. Yet the intense interest of those years in the environment, civil rights, and urban problems has faded. Will the concern over education policy be as short-lived as the rush of awareness that marked these earlier "crises"?

Just as politics gives us predictable cycles of reform, so media attention to those issues that arouse public attention helps to explain the repeated rediscovery of old problems, such as poverty, foreign competition, and low academic standards. These problems build up for many years, largely unnoticed by policymakers or the public. Then follows a period of alarmed discovery in the media, triggered usually by some signal event, in this case the report of the National Commission on Excellence in Education. A flurry of intense publicity follows, with national magazine cover stories and major news conferences.

After the initial flurry of activity, the public realizes how expensive and how difficult it will be to change something as fundamental as

The early 1980s have brought a period of disillusionment with professionals in general and educators in particular.

education, the environment, or our cities. Once this difficulty becomes apparent, the media, and with it public attention, begin to move on to other pressing issues. The next stage is the development of a few showy, superficial programs to remedy what are deep-seated and long-lasting problems, continuing loss of media attention, and a routinization of policy in the direction of traditional patterns. What we have, in short, is a disturbing tendency to overstress current or emerging media issues and to neglect fundamental solutions. Soon we shall see education lose the center of the media stage to be replaced by another issue, such as water quality, or the decaying infrastructure, or child abuse.

Equity *and* Excellence

But each of these cycles does leave some lasting improvement in public policy; all the furor is not without effect. Our task during this 1983-85 cycle will be to make some fundamental changes in our public education system. The launching of Sputnik in the autumn of 1957 not only sparked a tremendous surge of interest in science, foreign languages, mathematics, and a better curriculum for academically gifted students, but caused the federal government to intensify its role in education. Between 1957 and 1960, however, policymakers showed little concern for equity or for disadvantaged children. By the mid-1960s concern with civil rights and poverty reversed these priorities. The federal government eliminated its math and science summer institutes for teachers; enrollment in foreign languages and sciences plummeted; but black students' elementary school attainment rose.

The National Science Foundation budget to promote math and science in elementary and secondary education was phased out in 1981, only to be revived in 1983 because of the "Japanese competition" crisis. Education through work experience was discouraged and viewed as nonacademic. If the present Japanese competition cycle follows the Sputnik pattern, the issues featured in 1983, such as increased high school graduation requirements, will receive intense scrutiny, while in turn we neglect the groups that have made gains toward an equal opportunity for education within the last 15 years— women, the handicapped, the ethnic and racial minorities. If we do, we can predict that in the 1990s another group of national reports will probably decry the neglect of dropouts, the disadvantaged, the handicapped—all those with special needs—and will call, correctly, for an end to a national policy that underemphasizes equity.

What is needed is a policy that fights for both goals—excellence and equity—while balancing the claims of each. If either goal becomes the sole focus of policy a counterreaction will surely ensue. In pursuit of the goal of equity, leaders of education in the Carter administration encouraged bilingual instruction. In their zeal, they went so far as to specify the very classroom techniques to be used, offending state and local authorities who supported the goal of equity but found the federal regulations excessively detailed. The counterreaction came with the Reagan administration, which rescinded those directives and has moved against other parts of the equity agenda as well.

The 1983 Reports on Education

Although the differences among these reports have received considerable attention, more striking than their differences are their similarities in themes and prescriptions. All 1983 reports agree that the schools are spread over too many objectives. Our educational institutions, they contend, need to order their priorities. The high school curriculum, they assert, is fragmented and unregulated: They recommend that it focus on a common core of subjects—writing, science, mathematics—as a necessary step toward building the higher order skills of analysis and critical reasoning. (The key reports and critiques of the reports are listed in the notes.)

The reports agree that teacher training should be revised; that there should be more emphasis on subject matter, better approaches to teaching methods—and a career path. At present, a job description of the second year of teaching applies equally well to the fifteenth year. The reports stress that teachers need a career ladder that will provide different duties and levels of pay as a teacher's career develops. For students, the reports recommend more homework and more stringent requirements for high school graduation.

Although all the reports assert the primacy of the state and local roles in guiding education, they also call for a new partnership between the high schools, business, and higher education. For example, they urge the colleges to make clear their expectations about the content of courses in college preparatory subjects like English literature. All carry an undertone of concern for the nation's economic prosperity. That "rising tide of mediocrity . . . threatens America's ability to compete in world markets." We will lose our competitive edge to the Japanese and other countries, they warn, if education is not improved. This presumed link between education and economic growth has been crucial in catapulting education to the center stage of the media.

Most of the reports imply that education's promise to the public has been broken: Educators have been remiss in preparing students for college and for work; the schools have not lived up to the many and varied expectations held for them by society. Although the validity of this claim is a subject I shall discuss later, I want here to voice my concern about the absence of historical context in these reports. Lacking a grounding in history, they may initiate a mere repetition of past reform cycles, cycles during which we emphasized a few functions of the schools and neglected others, made superficial and ephemeral changes, and did not rethink the multiple objectives for our schools.

A study of high school reform cycles from 1890 to the present indicates that during periods of conservative political movements such as those of the 1890s, the late 1950s, and the early 1980s, discussions of education have focused on academic standards and traditional subjects like English, math, and history. But during periods of economic liberalism or progressive movements, such as the Depression and the 1960s, the focus has been on opportunity, equality, and vocational preparation—that is, on expanding the functions of the schools and on concern for disadvantaged minorities.

The current spate of national reports reflects yet another cycle of higher priority for traditional academic subjects, but it probably will not lead to fundamental reforms unless we resolve to limit our objectives and refocus our curriculum on fewer goals. Marginal change, such as adding five or ten days to the school calendar, will cost billions of dollars for only very slight improvement. The study of history also reveals a danger: We should be on the alert for the either/or syndrome, driven by the issue-attention cycle of the media. Although all the 1983 reports mention that our institutions of education must pursue equality and quality simultaneously, equality gets much less play in the current reports.

Beyond the Reports

While I am somewhat critical of these reports for their lack of historical perspective, I feel they have done us a national service in highlighting many of the genuine problems facing public education. If we do not succeed during the next few years in redeeming public confidence in our schools and restoring the image of quality performance, we will see more lobbying for public aid to private education through vouchers or tuition tax credits. The movement to seek private alternatives will grow, and the nation that invented free public education for all may turn aside from its own tradition.

But why do we still need public schools? We don't have to look far for the answers. In the last decade, some 7.5 million immigrants entered the United States, a number exceeded only by the 9 million who entered in the peak decade of 1900-1910. (In no other decade has immigration exceeded 5.2 million.) The need to teach community values and concepts to these newcomers is just as urgent as it was at the turn of the century, when our common schools began to fulfill their goals of free education for all. If the public schools do not embrace the vast majority of our children, then the only common transmitter of our culture is television. And thus far, television has not been a positive influence on American youth. One of the most popular programs on TV, for example, is *Dallas*, a serial that denigrates social ethics and emphasizes lying, cheating, and violence.

But there is an even stronger rationale for renewing our commitment to the public schools. The early promoters of public education sought a consensus that could lead to common action, not the separatist

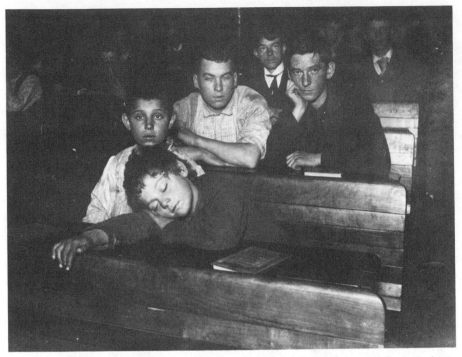

Jacob Riis, " Night School in Seventh Avenue Lodging Home" (Children's Aid Society) about 1900.

mentality of a sect. Horace Mann called for a larger loyalty that could dissolve apparent conflicts (as similar concepts of faith could draw together disparate Protestant sects). At a time when we have lost much of the national cohesiveness that the common school crusaders helped create, some critics of our schools would lead us to a system of government-assisted private and pluralistic schools. But such private schools

> would reinforce in the most restrictive fashion the political, ideological, and religious views of the family. That is, the school will be treated as a strict extension of the home, with little opportunity for students to experience the diversity of backgrounds and viewpoints that contribute to the democratic process.[3]

The study of attitudes toward dissent among West German youths, from which the above quotation is taken, supports this position. Those students who demonstrated a high tolerance for different viewpoints had been exposed to controversy or conflict to a greater extent than those who had little tolerance for dissenting views. From this restrictive tendency of private (often religious) schools derives one of the traditionally strongest arguments for public schools: That the state owes it to a child to provide some view of the world other than that of his or her parents. It is unlikely that Catholic schools will promote discussions of the pros and cons of birth control or that segregated white "academies" will work to overcome students' negative stereotypes of Blacks.

A school system that fosters no commitment to the common good is floundering in an excess of pluralism. We have gone too far in eliminating civic virtue and common values from the curriculum in recent years. What passes for values clarification in our public schools is more confusion than clarification and fails to address issues such as peaceful resolution of disputes. In values clarification courses students are asked to devise their own values rather than being led to understand those common values that Americans have held for centuries. The prescription, however, should not be structural change in the direction of promoting private schools through public funds; what we need is public school curricular reform. Shared values are the basis of shared goals, which have helped build collaboration and some crucial consensual elements for American society. Our public schools can still be what they have been for the last hundred years—key institutions in the formation and transmission of a common culture.

CHAPTER

THE COMMON SCHOOL— ITS ESTABLISHMENT AND REFORM

We Americans have long accommodated ourselves and our institutions to stresses arising from conflicts of values. In fact, we have made these stresses work to our benefit. The first, and still the best, commentator on American political life, Alexis de Tocqueville, noted the effect of what he considered a curious contradiction in our fundamental values. Traveling about the United States in the 1830s, de Tocqueville observed the clash between individualist and collectivist impulses in American life and concluded that this conflict made for a vital dynamism within the young democracy.

Certainly, individualism is reflected in our economic processes, our record of violence, and the restlessness of spirit characterizing the westward migration in the 1800s and the city migration of the 1900s. It is evident in the bills of rights in our national and state constitutions and, by extension, in the numerous devices to protect minority rights— for example, the requirement that school tax levies pass by a two-thirds majority.

The collectivist principle is seen in the special authority of popular majorities in our democracy. If all persons are regarded as important, the system must respond to their wishes. But because people's wishes are many and often conflicting, if democracy is to prevail, government must regulate conflicts so that they remain within tolerable limits. The operating principle of such regulation is that a given policy will take the direction preferred by the majority. Given the weight of each of these principles, the conflict between minority rights and majority rule is endemic to our democracy.

Until the nineteenth century, the harnessing of education to shape the political and religious order was typical of sovereign states. The state or nation shaped the school's function and purpose; the school did not shape or guide the state's. Education for the pursuit of other than approved ends, political and religious, was unknown. Although the development of private education in this country, with its implication of independence from the dictates of the state, originated in the desire to be free, "free" meant at liberty to inculcate the "right" religion without any interference from a central governmental authority. In colonial Massachusetts, the first schooling law was known as the "Old Deluder Satan Act," indicating that the Bible would be a keystone of the curriculum and that the purpose of education was to teach the young how to evade Satan's snares.

In a democratic society, the relationship of the schools to the state is particularly complicated, for the schools must manage tensions between opposing values even as they support the state. Like the conflict between majority rule and minority rights, the conflict between individualism and patriotic loyalty is inherent in the system. The American public school must teach a reasonable measure of loyalty to the state; it must also teach the virtues of American individualism. And individualism can lead to opposition to the state, as our recent history of civil protest and violence attests.

Egalitarianism versus Individualism

Tension between support of the state and encouragement of individualism is a major source of conflict over school policy. But it is hardly the only source. The breadth of our democratic values makes serious conflicts unavoidable. For example, one of the norms of citizenship in our society is egalitarianism, a belief that all citizens should possess equal rights and equal opportunities—"With liberty and justice for all," as schoolchildren say in the Pledge of Allegiance. In 1976, the year of our bicentennial celebration, two national surveys, one of 13-year-olds and one of 17-year-olds, found this value to be deeply rooted. A huge majority of the young people surveyed opposed discrimination in the job market—racial (96 percent), religious (97 percent), political (82 percent in one group and 92 in the other), and sexual (87 percent).

Yet in educational policy, egalitarianism generates conflict when it challenges and is challenged by other potent values. Among these is another version of concern for individual and minority rights—re-

Town and country schools were designed for the same end: to give pupils a basic elementary education that would fit them for participation in political life and for entrance into the world of work.

gionalism or localism, in the form of local control of educational policy. Local control of the school has been a dominant value in our history for over a century (since 1850), and so has the concept of equal educational opportunity. Since 1954, these principles have collided head on over the issue of racial segregation, as the federal government's actions on behalf of equality have restricted the power of local school districts. In that year, the Supreme Court rejected the "separate but equal" doctrine under which school boards in the South had maintained racially segregated schools. In *Brown v. Board of Education*, the Supreme Court ruled that segregated schools were inherently unequal.

It may well be that the centrifugal pull of individualism has been checked by our tendency to live and socialize mostly with those who agree with us. In much of our past, American society has consisted of islands of conformity, each oriented to different values and indifferent to or unaware of the others. The Bible Belt schools ignored

evolution, while urban northern schools treated it fully; rural Protestant schools might require prayers, while urban liberal enclaves
ignored them. Not for us the French school system in which at a given
hour every child of a given age in every school is learning the same
thing.

Still another basic American value helps us to manage our conflicts,
to make them a source of dynamism rather than of destruction. That
value is pragmatism, a characteristically American preference for a
practical rather than a theoretical approach. We see pragmatism in
the constant shaping of the curriculum to meet special concerns—in
farm, industrial, and military training classes, for example. Pragmatism shows everywhere in the early history of American education,
for what worked well at one site was soon transmitted elsewhere.
Working together with individualism and respect for majority rule,
American pragmatism—undeterred by bonds of the past, stimulated
by the challenge of a new society, and mobilizing collective mutual
interest—has provided a crystallizing value. Our school policies illustrate this blend of individualism, or localism, majoritarianism, and
pragmatism.

The Common School Movement

At the founding of the republic, formal education for young people
was not a universally shared goal. Indeed, many reasons existed for
opposing the establishment of public schools. Echoes of these are heard
today among advocates of education vouchers or tuition tax credits,
who want public funding for private schools in the belief that school
should be an extension of the home, where children will encounter
only the values espoused by like-minded families. Along the way,
though, many Americans did accept the idea of a common school. We
tend to take for granted the signs of this acceptance at every level of
social organization, among them the national commitment to use land
sales to finance schools and colleges, formalized in the Northwest
Ordinance of 1787 and the Morrill Land Acts of 1862 and 1890; the
states' commitment to provide free public access to education—at first
to the grammar school only, then to high school, and now to junior
or community colleges; and the local communities' efforts to finance
free extra-curricular activities such as football, debating, band, and
chess club. Throughout our history, however, the belief that "education
is a good thing" has had different meanings viewed from each of the
pluralist perspectives of our society. Early on, education was consid-

A sod schoolhouse in Nebraska. The young teacher holds a bell as a symbol of her authority.

ered important for religious training. Eventually, the American people decided that education should be available to all *and* that public funds should not be provided to private schools in any appreciable amount.

The school, as we know it, is a product of the common school movement of the mid-nineteenth century, a vast social movement that spread a basically similar institution from coast to coast across a sparsely settled continent. In 1860, 80 percent of Americans lived in rural areas; there was no United States Office of Education and only the tiniest beginning of state educational bureaucracies. Indeed, as late as 1890, the median size of state departments of education was two, including the state superintendent. Now the California State Department of Education, for example, has about 3,100 employees.

Today, when public education is so familiar a part of our lives, it is hard to recapture the ambience of the pre–Civil War era, when the common school was still a tenuous experiment. Prior to the movement, Americans supported all kinds of schools. But it was the genius of the common school crusaders like Horace Mann and many Protestant ministers to persuade citizens that American millennial destiny was best served by support of a common school. Hundreds of thousands of such promoters from Maine to Oregon accomplished this task, not a central ministry of education. By the Civil War, the common school was already the mainstream of schooling in the United States. In the idea of a common school, the values of egalitarianism and majoritarianism played a significant part.

In general, lay people built and supervised the public schools, and young, untrained teachers instructed the pupils. As advocated by Mann and others, the common school was to include children from all classes, sects, and ethnic groups. It existed to produce literate, numerate, and moral citizens. Theoretically nonsectarian and nonpartisan in politics, the common school often had a Protestant and conservative slant. Nonetheless, most citizens, with the exception of Roman Catholics, found its teachings inoffensive. (While Roman Catholics constituted a considerable exception, in the late nineteenth century they made up only 10 percent of the population.)

The promoters of public education were Victorian opinion shapers, largely British-American in ethnic origin, bourgeois in economic outlook and status, and evangelically Protestant in religious orientation. They believed that a common school, controlled and financed largely by local trustees and public taxation, was essential to the realization of a millennial vision of a righteous republic. In the United States, Protestants joined together as they did not in England, for example, to support the public school, and political parties did not differ in their educational programs to any significant degree. The creation of such a system was an undertaking of immense magnitude—indeed, the greatest institution-building success in American history.

Values Nurtured by the Common School

The Protestant-republican ideology embodied in this institution was vividly expressed by the *McGuffey Readers*, first published in 1836 and used by some 200 million schoolchildren from 1900 to 1940 (their use began to fade in the 1920s). The *Readers* were frankly moralistic. In story after story good children are rewarded (soon after their good deeds and with solid items like silver coins), while bad ones are punished with equal celerity. Honesty and industry are the leading values, closely followed by courage, kindness, obedience, and courtesy. The *Readers* supported the temperance movement but were silent about the movements to abolish slavery and to establish trade unions. Their content is varied, including selections from literature, British as well as American, and lessons in science, farming, history, and bi-

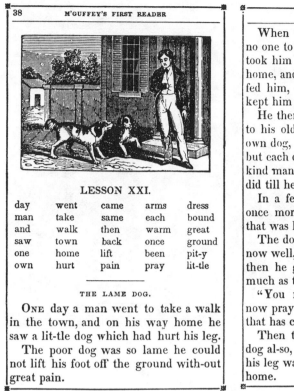

LESSON XXI.

day	went	came	arms	dress
man	take	same	each	bound
and	walk	then	warm	great
saw	town	back	once	ground
one	home	lift	been	pit-y
own	hurt	pain	pray	lit-tle

THE LAME DOG.

ONE day a man went to take a walk in the town, and on his way home he saw a lit-tle dog which had hurt his leg.

The poor dog was so lame he could not lift his foot off the ground with-out great pain.

When this kind man saw there was no one to take pit-y on the poor dog, he took him in his arms, and brought him home, and bound up his leg. Then he fed him, and made a warm place, and kept him in his house for two days.

He then sent the dog out of his house, to his old home; for, as it was not his own dog, he had no right to keep him; but each day the dog came back for this kind man to dress his leg. And this he did till he was quite well.

In a few weeks the dog came back once more, and with him came a dog that was lame.

The dog that had been lame, and was now well, first gave the man a look, and then he gave the lame dog a look, as much as to say:

"You made my lame leg well, and now pray do the same for this poor dog that has come with me."

Then the kind man took care of this dog al-so, and kept him in his house till his leg was quite well, and he could go home.

The lesson in kindness typifies the moralistic tone of the *McGuffey Readers*.

ography. Parson Weems's tale of George Washington and the cherry tree is there—"I can't tell a lie, Father, you know I can't tell a lie. I cut it with my hatchet"—and a capsule history of the United States. The *Readers* also presented serious or philosophical topics, such as religion, the value of education, and death (in the family or on the battlefield).

From the one-room school of rural communities to the graded school of towns and cities, town and country schools were designed for the same end: To give pupils a basic elementary education that would fit them for participation in political life and for entrance into the world of work. If, in succeeding decades, we have added many objectives to an originally quite limited curriculum, the rationale for such additions was already established. Courses in bookkeeping, surveying, industrial drawing, and commercial skills, at first taught in proprietary

Students exercising in the classroom, Brockton, Massachusetts, circa 1903.

schools (private, profit-making vocational schools) moved into the public schools in the decades from 1845 to 1865. Catharine Beecher, devoted to secondary education for women, wrote textbooks on domestic economy so that young women might master the economic skills of their sphere—homemaking.

Henry Barnard, another nineteenth-century leader of education, believed, and persuaded others to believe, that the school should inculcate positive rules of healthful living, among these, the dangers of tobacco and liquor. Catharine Beecher, for her part, urged that the school teach the importance of fresh air, loose clothing, simple diet, and exercise.

Intellect, health, and character equally concerned the nineteenth-century educator. Many leaders in education considered the school superior to the home as a source of values and moral training, and superior, certainly, to society at large, which offered the young the temptations of the street. By the teacher's example and the moral precepts that pervaded the textbooks, the school was to shape children to a pan-Protestant morality and a politically neutral form of republican virtue. [1] Those who believe that "back to basics" means a return to a nineteenth-century model of schools focused wholly upon the development of the intellect have mistaken the nature of nineteenth-century schooling.

School Board Politics

While the common school movement established a fairly uniform national system of schools, a still more powerful nationalizing force has been of greater consequence over a longer period: the force of professionalism. The growth of professional standards for administration, teaching, curriculum, testing, and other elements essential to the system drew it together during the final decades of the last century. Before this unifying process emerged, the fabric of American schools was still plaid, and a ragged plaid at that. Experience drawn from the testing of a jumble of ideas, ideas transmitted through new professional journals and new training for the emergent profession, did far more than the political system or the common school movement to impose a striking uniformity on American instructional practices. In this movement toward centralization, the value of pragmatism played a large part, together with a closely associated value—efficiency.

At the turn of the century (1890-1910) municipal corruption was everywhere—in the schools as in the city offices. Muckrakers exposed textbook publishers and contractors who allied themselves with corrupt school trustees for common boodle in the common school. Leaders concerned about these practices in big cities gathered information from across the country. Their reports indicted every region of the country.

> A superintendent in one of the Eastern states writes: "Nearly all the teachers in our schools get their positions by political 'pull.' If they secure a place and are not backed by political influence, they are likely to be turned out. Our drawing teacher recently lost her position for this reason." One writes from the South: "Most places depend on politics. The lowest motives are frequently used to influence ends." A faint wail comes from the far West: "Positions are secured and held by the lowest principles of corrupt politicians." "Politicians wage a war of extermination against all teachers who are not their vassals," comes from the Rocky Mountains.

In Boston, the teachership is still a spoil of office. It is more difficult, at the present time, for a Catholic than for a Protestant young woman to get a place, but, nevertheless, some Catholics secure appointments, for "trading" may always be done, while each side has a wholesome fear of the other assailing it in the open board. A member said one day, in my hearing: "I must have my quota of teachers."[2]

The situation was reinforced with a vengeance by local control. A ward-based, decentralized committee system for administering the public schools provided opportunities for extensive political influence. In 1905, Philadelphia had 43 elected district school boards with 559 members. The Cincinnati school board had 74 subcommittees, while Chicago had 79. The Minneapolis school board had only seven members, but Hartford, Connecticut, with a third the population, had 39.

Centralization of Control

Reformers contended that board members elected by wards advanced their own parochial and special interests at the expense of the school district as a whole. What was needed to counter this atomization, they believed, was election at large or citywide without any subdistrict electoral boundaries. A good school system was good for everyone, not for just one segment of the community. Reformers also charged that the executive authority of the larger school boards was splintered because they worked through subcommittees. In 1910, no topic, from how to teach reading to the purchase of doorknobs, was too complex or too trivial for a separate subcommittee to consider. The basic prerequisite for better management was thought to be centralization of power in a chief executive to whom the selection board would delegate considerable authority. The school superintendent would be controlled, but only on very broad policies, by a board respectful of his professional expertise. Only under such a system could a superintendent make large-scale improvements and be held accountable.

By 1910 a conventional educational wisdom had evolved among the schoolfolk and leading business and professional men who had spearheaded the reforms. The reformers sought to use state legislatures and departments of education to standardize public education and consolidate one-room schools into larger township or regional schools. Essentially, they aimed to "take education out of politics"—meaning, usually, away from decentralized control by lay people—and to turn "political" issues into matters for administrative discretion by professional educators. Sometimes only a very small group of patricians secured new charters from state legislatures and thereby reorganized the urban schools without any popular vote. The watchwords of reform were efficiency, expertise, professionalism, centralization, and nonpolitical control. Taken together, reformers thought, these ideals would inspire the "one best system."[3]

Professionalism and the Middle Class

The most attractive models for this new structure of organization and governance were the large industrial corporate bureaucracies emerging rapidly in the turn-of-the-century economy. The centralized power of the superintendent, comparable to that of the plant manager, was supposed to overcome the tangles and inefficiencies of school board subcommittees. The appeal of the industrial model came from another source as well—from the social class and status of the reformers. The financial and professional leaders who deplored the politics and inefficiency of the decentralized ward system had another reason for disliking that system: It empowered members of the lower and lower-middle classes, many of whom were recent working-class immigrants. Reformers wanted "not simply to replace bad men with good; they proposed to change the occupational and class origins of the decision makers."[4]

After these reforms were enacted, membership on governing agencies did in fact change. A classic study done in 1927 showed that upper-class professionals and business people made up the newly organized centralized boards of education.[5] For instance, in Saint Louis, after reforms in 1897, the percentage of professionals on the board jumped from 4.8 percent to 58.3 percent and that of big businessmen from 9 percent to 25 percent. In contrast, the percentage of small businessmen dropped from 47.6 percent to 16.7 percent, and that of wage earners from 28.6 percent to none. These professional and managerial board members delegated many of their formal powers to professionals in education, thus granting to educators the discretion to shape schools to meet the needs of industrial society—as defined by one segment of that society, chiefly prosperous, native-born, Protestant Anglo-Saxons. At this point the country had a consensus on school policy and a limited set of functions for the schools.

FIGURE 3-1

High School Graduates as a Percentage of the U.S. Population, Aged 17, 1920–50

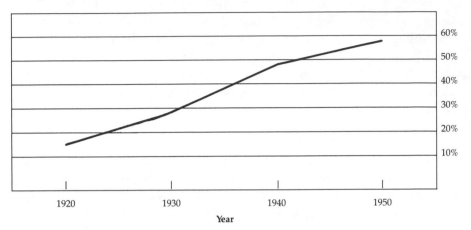

Source: *Historical Statistics of the U.S.*, vol. I, p. 379.

But policy did not reflect American pluralism, and only 16 percent of the population graduated from high school in 1920 (see Figure 3-1).

The Rise of Vocational Education

Between 1910 and 1930, waves of immigration from Europe were changing the country and with it the secondary school curriculum. High school enrollment expanded, and throughout the school system, especially in the urban centers, students appeared whose parents were industrial workers. The apprentice system had been declining, and the country had need of a dependable supply of skilled labor capable of building and repairing machinery (just as now the economy is said to need "computer-literate" workers). If now we seem preoccupied with Japanese schooling and its relation to Japan's economic success, in the late nineteenth century the model for the United States was Germany. German vocational schools were greatly admired, and the National Association of Manufacturers urged that America, too, establish trade schools. The NAM concerned itself with workers' attitudes as well as with skills. The public system of education was asked to serve the nation by inculcating positive attitudes toward work and by training students in specific skills and processes.

Idealistic middle-class reformers, too, focused upon vocational education, but from another perspective, the individualistic perspective of the young people who found themselves bored and unhappy in

Vocational courses like industrial drawing, at first taught in private, profit-making schools, moved into the public schools in the decades from 1845 to 1865. Later, the National Association of Manufacturers lobbied for the establishment of trade schools. In 1918 the Smith-Hughes Act established vocational education in the secondary schools.

dead-end jobs. These reformers concerned themselves with the choice of vocation, and from their efforts developed programs in vocational guidance, career awareness, work experience, and cooperative training between the school and the employer. With the school boards now heavily weighted with prosperous business and professional people, a coalition formed between associations of business people, members of Congress, school board members, and reformers; this was the powerful coalition that established vocational education and vocational guidance as staples of public schooling.

In 1918 the Smith-Hughes Act established vocational education in the secondary schools. With federal government funding, programs in vocational education grew steadily from an enrollment of 164,000 in 1918 to 8.79 million in 1970. At present, vocational educators are a well-organized lobby with branches at the national, state, and local level. They are allied with the Future Farmers of America, the 4H clubs, and agribusiness, as well as with the NAM.

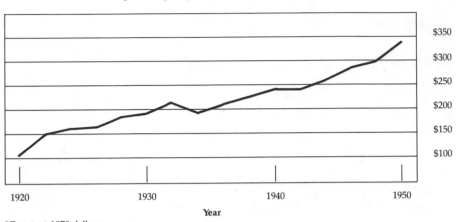

FIGURE 3-2
Current Operating Expenditures per Pupil, 1920–50*

*Constant 1970 dollars.
Source: Historical Statistics of the U.S., vol. I, pp. 373–374.

The commitment to public education has held firm even in times of economic stress. Only in the bleakest years of the early Depression (1931–35) did school expenditures per pupil drop. By 1936, the upward spending trend resumed.

Through a committee of the National Education Association, the consensus that established vocational education expressed its views: In 1918, leading professional educators formulated "The Cardinal Principles of Secondary Education." Their aim was to broaden the curriculum in high schools and thereby attract and retain a larger number of students. The "Cardinal Principles" enshrined, as the chief objective of the school curriculum, preparation of the young for social life, that is, "for health, worthy home membership, vocation, citizenship, worthy use of leisure time, and ethical character."[6] The men who formulated these goals trusted to efficiency and expertise; they were "social engineers." In the phrase "worthy use of leisure time," the individualist and idealistic strain of educational philosophy asserts itself as well.

The Depression Years

The most surprising outcome of the Depression Era of 1930-41 was that this terrible economic era did not severely change the commitment to public education.[7] For example, only in the bleakest years of the early depression (1931-35) did school expenditures per pupil drop; by 1936 the upward spending trend resumed (see Figure 3-2). The trend

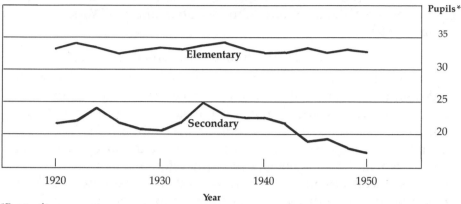

FIGURE 3-3
Pupil-Teacher Ratio in Public Schools, 1920–50

*Per teacher.

Source: Historical Statistics of the U.S., vol. I, p. 368.

During the Depression Era (1931–40) the national commitment to public education was renewed. In spite of economic hardships, the number of teachers grew at a faster rate than the number of students.

toward broadening the curriculum continued, spurred by the egalitarian social concerns of the period. The number of teachers grew faster than the numbers of pupils during the Depression, particularly at the secondary level (see Figure 3-3). This costly increase in the ratio of teachers to pupils took place despite a sharp rise in high school attendance. Youngsters, unable to find work, stayed in school—a trend reinforced by a growing conviction among parents that secondary schooling would help their children obtain better jobs. The enactment of compulsory schooling laws and the banning of child labor by the states also contributed to the expanded enrollment.

The Depression Era was also a time of educational innovation characterized by the "progressive" approach. Progressives opposed the traditional format—children sitting in their seats reciting as they were called on. They favored putting children to work at projects, allowing them to learn by doing; they encouraged critical questioning, movement of pupils around the classroom. But this classroom experimentation was not accompanied by challenges to the inequalities that were deeply embedded in the schools. Schools mirrored the larger society: They were sharply divided by race, class, and gender. Blacks were segregated, women tracked into dead-end vocations, and school districts with little local property wealth were bereft of basic school resources like buildings and trained teachers. The most dramatic efforts to ameliorate the economic deprivation of the nation's youth took place outside of public schools through such New Deal programs as the National Youth Administration and the Works Progress Administration.

The Curriculum Grows Broader

During the period of economic expansion and social change that followed World War II, the curriculum adapted, as the society did, to peacetime social life and economic expansion. The number of students enrolled in school and the percentage graduating from high school continued to increase. The egalitarianism of the army encouraged egalitarianism in the schools, even in heretofore elitist institutions—the private colleges and universities—as thousands of ex-soldiers enrolled in college with the help of the federal government under the G.I. Bill. The curriculum continued to expand to meet the needs of an even greater variety of students.

The schools were also engaged to serve society at large by helping individuals make the transition from war to peace. The goal of the "life adjustment" programs of the 1940s, as of the "Cardinal Principles" of 1918, was to imbue the entire school curriculum with a practical ideology, to downplay academic learning, and to fit the happy individual to the peaceful group. A text on citizenship published in 1953 illustrates the extreme of this view. It included sections on "how to be a good follower," "how to get your share of the family car," and "how to take part in school songs and yells."[8]

The era from 1920 to 1950 was a "golden era" for school superintendents, who had a great deal of discretion and no teachers' unions to worry about. Federal and state governments were content to let decisions rest with local authorities. The turn-of-the-century triumph of the doctrine of efficiency achieved through professionalism and centralization attenuated the ties between school leadership and its constituents. Parent participation had little impact on school policy making. As the leading citizens' "interest group," the PTA considered its prime function to be the providing of support for the policies of professional administrators.

Until the 1950s, Baltimore held its school board meetings in a room that seated only 25 people. This weakened linkage between the professional leadership and the community was acceptable in the pre-World War II decades when schooling made lesser claims on community financial resources—and when professionals benefited from their own publicity about education as the sovereign key to success. It continued to be acceptable in the two decades after the war, when emphasis was on the rush to obtain schooling for all. But school politics were about to change, and in several directions at once. The efficiency of the centralized professional administration was losing its aura, and new ways of both elitism and egalitarianism were to overtake educational policy.

CHAPTER

4

FROM SPUTNIK TO THE WAR ON POVERTY

Sometime during the late 1950s, confidence in school administrators and local school boards began to fade. In 1954, the *Brown* decision outlawing statutory school segregation called attention to the disgraceful failure of southern educators and school boards to educate their black students. Other weaknesses were revealed: Regardless of race, Johnny and Jane could not read or speak foreign languages or calculate in base ten. After the launching of Sputnik in 1957, an angry chorus complained that the Russian system of education was out-performing our own. Our rivalry with the Soviet Union galvanized a more aggressive federal role in education in the form of the National Defense Education Act passed in the late 1950s, which laid the ground-work for federal support of university education in the early 1960s and the $1.5 billion Elementary and Secondary Education Act in 1965, a central feature of President Lyndon Johnson's War on Poverty and his program for a "great society." The National Defense Education Act of 1957 emphasized math, science, and foreign languages to meet Soviet competition—the same priority we have fixed on in 1984 to strengthen us against Japanese industrial competition.

The 1965 federal aid expansion reflected a dominant concern with civil rights, big city riots, and the elimination of poverty. Federal programs were earmarked for reducing the persistent inequalities that state and local policymakers tolerated. Federal aid peaked in 1970 at 9 percent of the total expenditure for schools; it is currently 7 percent. The "target groups" remain the same—low-income minorities, women, handicapped children, limited-English-speaking immigrants, and the rural poor. The federal courts have led in abolishing racial and gender discrimination (measured by expenditure and curricular opportunities) and in establishing the right to an education for handicapped children. In the 1970s, federal court decisions mandated that high schools cease to track women into sex-stereotyped occupations. The overwhelming majority of women were being tracked into vocational programs such as nursing, waitress training, and secretarial work. These legal mandates were a stimulus for Title IX of the Civil Rights Act, which prohibits sex discrimination in funding at all levels of education. The expansion of women's intercollegiate sports is one of the happy results of this policy.

Parent Constituencies and "Participation"

The more voters and taxpayers contributed to education, however, the more they complained as parents that the educational bureaucracy was not sensitive to their preferences in schooling their children. Social scientists joined in the grumbling with analyses of the monolithic— that is, unresponsive—nature of the schooling administration. New York City's remote and impenetrable central headquarters at 110 Livingston Street came to be regarded by critics as the archetype of school administration rather than as an aberrant exception. Suburbanites maintained that administrators were insensitive to their demands for either richer or plainer curricula, whether in affluent Scarsdale, New York, or working-class Maple Heights, Ohio. In the central cities, particularly in the newly mobilized black communities, central offices and school principals were increasingly attacked for their insensitivity, often labeled racism. Across a surprisingly wide range of social groups, parents-as-voters were moved to criticize their lack of connection with school district decision making.

The watchword for these aroused groups of parent-taxpayers became "participation." During the 1970s, notions of shared control took on new forms. Sometimes participation involved a formal structure through which parents could have a say in school decisions, and parental advisory committees were established at the level of the school site. In California, for example, community members joined the principal and teachers of the school to set a significant part of the budget in accordance with their own definition of good education. In Chicago, parental committees came to have a large, though not definitive, role in evaluating principals' professional behavior.

To meet individual needs arising from students' ethnic backgrounds, bilingual programs were introduced in the 1970s.

Parents also acted upon their opinions about what was taught in the classroom. During the 1950s, some parents had voiced their fear that the schools were teaching communism. In the 1970s others vented their anger against teachers who taught biological evolution or assigned fiction containing harsh language or critical views of American society. Other parents rose to defend the same curriculum subjects. These battles found expression in street demonstrations, court suits, and state legislative lobbies, all accompanied by a steady vilification of professionals and school board members. At their worst, these disputes led to violence. In the mid-1970s, in Kanawha county, West Virginia, opposition to the teaching of a social studies curriculum called "Man: A Course of Study" prompted the dynamiting of the school district's central office.

Parents challenged the effectiveness of the schooling process—as measured by academic achievement. The earlier dissatisfaction with students' low reading skills evolved into increasing claims (supported by some data) that schools were not teaching effectively. By the late seventies and early eighties national news magazines were featuring articles on these school "failures." There have been demands that teachers be held individually responsible for their pupils' progress, and by the end of the 1970s some states had moved to require examination of teachers—in some instances to determine the effectiveness of their classroom teaching, in others to test the adequacy of their basic education and training. The authority that had been traditionally granted school professionals was being challenged—and confidence and trust in education eroded.

Many of the ideals and achievements of the administrators active between 1920 and 1950 have been sharply attacked over the last two decades. The ideal of a "closed" political system in equilibrium run primarily by school superintendents and their experts has been shaken, and many new groups have entered the decision-making process. Members of minorities have pressed for structural changes, primarily for desegregation, for community control, and for curricular additions such as black history or bilingual instruction. "Decentralizers" in cities have sought to reinstitute something resembling the old ward boards of education abolished during the decades from 1890 to 1920. Legal activists have challenged the use of I.Q. tests for pupil placement and tracking. (The I.Q. test was first used during the 1920s and illustrates the allegiance of that period to efficiency and expertise.)

Teachers Organize

The last 25 years have seen a decline in the collectivist and centralizing impulses. Individualism and loyalty to a group of one's own—defined, usually, by race, region, sex, age, or social position—have gained in attractive power. The last 25 years, especially the 1960s and 1970s, have seen the growth of multiple constituencies and the fragmentation of decision-making authority, with the results described in Chapter 2. Not least among the multiple constituencies entering the decision-making process during these decades are the teachers' organizations.

In the 1950s, teachers found themselves cut off from the school board and the public. Increasingly, they were being told how to conduct their classrooms by business managers, administrative assistants, subject-matter coordinators, and department heads. At the same time, as education became big business, teachers were achieving a potential for power. After World War II, more parents wanted their children to have more schooling and there were also more children to educate. The country then spent more on education, and more teachers were needed. Between 1949 and 1970, the share of the gross national product devoted to education rose from about 3.5 percent to 8 percent. Where we had spent only $2 billion in 1940, we spent $50 billion in 1970, and over $100 billion in 1980. With this massive injection of funds into the schools, teachers grew in numbers from just over one million in 1940 to almost 2.5 million in 1971. By the mid-1970s teachers were one million fewer in number than farmers but substantially more numerous than teamsters, auto workers, steelworkers, or doctors.

During the 1950s, the teachers' perception of their "proper professional role" began to change. Once viewed as submissive, they now began to form unions, to engage in collective bargaining, and—despite laws in many states against strikes by public employees—to use the tactic of the strike. The number of strikes escalated between 1955 and 1975, from 35 to 114 in the single school year 1967-68 and to 131 in 1969-70.

Teachers' organizations also entered into federal electoral politics. In 1976, the National Education Association (NEA) endorsed a presidential candidate—Jimmy Carter—and spent $3 million on behalf of their endorsed candidates in federal elections. Not surprisingly, in 1979 President Carter successfully pushed for a new cabinet-level Department of Education, something the NEA had much desired. An estimated 300 delegates to the Democratic convention in 1980 were NEA members, the largest interest block there, and again the NEA endorsed Carter. The rival teachers' organization, the American Federation of Teachers, sent 66 delegates to the convention, and endorsed another candidate. In 1980, the attempt of Carter's successful opponent, Ronald Reagan, to abolish the department was defeated by the Congress.

A teacher works with a deaf child. In 1970 over 3.1 million students were enrolled in special education programs for the handicapped. The federal courts have led the way in establishing the right to an education for handicapped children.

As teachers participate more fully in the reallocation of resources at the national, state, and local levels, they lose the aura they once had of being apolitical or above politics. It was this mythical quality that enabled them to claim a large share of resources for so long without having to contend with other claimants. Now, in the state legislatures and city councils, where school budgets are sometimes reviewed, teachers are only one more pressure group whose claim to special treatment must be balanced against others' claims.

Innovations

The period of reform starting in 1958 just after Sputnik and lasting to the mid-1970s was marked by kaleidoscopic change. The state of California alone mounted 52 different reform initiatives from 1958 to 1975. To cite even a few reform efforts is to suggest how diverse they were in philosophy and program: New curricula in science and mathematics were developed for gifted students, and compensatory education for "disadvantaged" students. Bilingual/bicultural programs and ethnic studies were a response to the requests of various minority groups, as were various kinds of provisions for handicapped students. Innovation became the watchword. Team teaching, open classrooms (where students moved about freely as they worked alone or in small groups), and performance-contracting between teacher and students were designed to motivate students and to inspire teachers. Programs were devised to develop the social character of students—affective education to raise their self-esteem, and sensitivity training to make them trusting toward and aware of the feelings of others. Still other programs aimed to heighten the egalitarian atmosphere of the school by eliminating sexual bias in athletics or vocational education. During this period, the number of programs in which federal money was earmarked for special purposes—from library books and lab equipment to physical therapy for handicapped students—grew to 66.

Youth Becomes a Constituency

What accounted for this rapid succession of innovations? For one thing, the *Brown* school desegregation decision of 1954 was being implemented. Schools were being desegregated, and, as the demands of the black minority received a favorable response, other minorities came forward to express their needs. Among the pressure groups to emerge were the students themselves. The early 1970s began with the rediscovery of "youth problems." As the Vietnam War triggered youth

In 1954 the Supreme Court ruled (in *Brown v. Board of Education*) that schools segregated by race were prohibited by the Fourteenth Amendment to the Constitution.

protests, students were seen to be alienated from schools and adults, and unmotivated in their studies. The salient policy goal was to allow students greater choice and to drop rigid requirements. Youth had become a constituency with demands to be met, and educators responded to these demands by offering students a flexible curriculum, independent study, and education off the school grounds, chiefly in the workplace—by which youth could presumably be drawn closer to adult values.

For the youth constituency, a key value was freedom of choice. The authors of *High School* (1971) listed three key problems facing the schools: Racism, authoritarianism, and the irrelevance of the curriculum. Of the last they wrote, "Students are insisting that the curricula grow out of their own interests and concerns, that they be permitted to choose which path to learning to take."[1] High school electives proliferated as students were given more opportunity to choose their courses. The English Department in a big-city high school expanded its course offerings from 20 to about 100, including science-fiction novels and individually designed mini-courses.

The Legacies of Reform

A further explanation for the accelerating pace of change or reform in education policy lies in the variety of functions—legacies of earlier reforms—the schools had come to serve. Through reform after reform and expansion upon expansion, our schools, and especially our comprehensive high schools, have come to resemble a vast social service agency. The school has become custodian of children and young people who would not have been enrolled at all a century ago, or even sixty years ago. In 1890 only 3.5 percent of 17-year-olds were graduated from high school; by 1970 the number had risen to 75.6 percent. In 1922, classes for the mentally retarded enrolled 23 thousand students; in 1970, 830 thousand; and in the same year over 3.1 million students were enrolled in special education programs for the handicapped.

In expanding so greatly, the schools of the country have become "nearly a universal institution." Most of us take for granted that primary and secondary schools have taken on roles once performed by families, churches, employers and fellow workers, and voluntary agencies like the YMCA. The services this encompassing system provides are familiar, yet David Tyack's listing of them is still impressive. Over time, the schools have come to provide

> lunches, dental and medical inspections, nursing care, physical education, health classes, playgrounds and recreation, psychological counseling and mental health facilities, student government and extra-curricular activities. . . . vocational courses and vocational guidance. Dozens of new positions appeared as a result of this specialization and extension of functions: teachers of driver education, home economics, or sheet metal work; counselors; curriculum or disciplinary vice-principals; school social workers; dieticians and lunchroom workers; nurses; social activity directors; and many others.[2]

The schools are custodians of youth. We don't like students to drop out of school before age 17; in too many cases, young children not in school are left on their own, and teenagers cannot find jobs. By 1990, over 60 percent of mothers with school-age children will have jobs. The school must be a safe place for children from early morning until late afternoon, when after-school extracurricular activities come to an end. In gradually assuming responsibility for the health and

Independence High School, San Jose, California, is the largest secondary school campus in California, with an enrollment of nearly 4,100 students on the 105-acre campus.

general welfare of youth, the schools have multiplied their objectives until what we now ask of the public schools goes beyond what they— or, perhaps, any single social institution—can reasonably hope to accomplish.

Our Overburdened Schools

Perhaps the most vivid way to illustrate the accretion of educational objectives over time is to list, briefly, the objectives we expect the schools to meet. I can list no fewer than nine.

1) To Impart Information and to Teach Intellectual Skills

We expect the schools to equip students with basic knowledge and to guide them in the development of intellectual skills, among them how to solve problems and, broadly, how to think. This ambitious aim embraces the traditional academic areas—language and literature, math, social studies, and science. Memorization of content is not enough. Our students should be able to solve math problems that are presented in forms other than those in their textbook exercises. They should be able to interpret complex literary works, and to analyze the tone and mood of the author. Their writing skills should encompass exposition and argumentation as well as simple statement.

2) To Transmit Social Values

We place special emphasis upon knowledge of our democracy, our heritage and values. If, indeed, a major rationale for establishing common schools was to transmit the common culture to what was then a nation of immigrants, we can demand no less for today's youth. They are to learn the essentials of our governmental system and to absorb centrally important values such as those embodied in the Bill of Rights and in the laws protecting property rights. Civic education and civic duty are included in this goal, and many states require instruction in the concepts of capitalist economics.

3) To Develop Individuality; To Nurture Creativity and Imagination

Even while we devote much time and energy to transmitting to students the intellectual and cultural heritage of our society, we ask the school to look upon each student as uniquely valuable and to help each discover his or her special skills and abilities. Programs for the gifted and classes in the arts and in music are designed to develop individual gifts and creative powers. In support of this project, many argue that unique individual creativity is more important than knowledge for making scientific as well as artistic breakthroughs. Fantasy and imagination are encouraged through activities like fingerpainting, dancing, creative writing, and a variety of extracurricular activities.

4) To Encourage Self-esteem

Just as we want the schools to develop and even to discover individual talent, we want them to strengthen the self-esteem and clarify the self-concept of every student. Many educators contend that children and young people need to understand feelings and how to deal with them as a primary path to self-actualization.

5) To Promote Good Health

In physical education and classes on nutrition we expect the schools to prepare students for a lifetime of sound habits. Specific curricular units on smoking, venereal disease, diet, and safe driving have been added to the store of information the school must transmit. In many schools the staff includes psychologists to promote students' emotional health.

6) To Provide Vocational Preparation

We also make the schools responsible for developing the saleable skills that will match the current and future needs of the job market. Comprehensive high schools have divisions for office occupations, auto repair, electronics assembly, and home-building.

7) To Prepare for Life and Leisure

Schools train future parents through courses in child development and ready the young for worthy use of leisure time through classes in photography, sewing, and crafts. To provide young people with homemaking skills, home economics and cooking courses have been integrated into the curricula of most secondary schools.

8) To Develop Moral Integrity

Schools are asked to transmit and strengthen societal values such as honesty, respect for those who are different, fairness (sharing equally), and rejection of violence or corruption. Churches are an important conduit of these values, but the public also expects the schools to take a major responsibility in this area.

9) To Separate and Select

Although we ask the schools to improve the self-esteem of each student, we also demand that the school system sort and sift, separating the achievers from those with limited potential for academic work. Students are tested and graded until they are sorted into two basic groups, the college-bound and those who will go to work right after high school. In moving through the school system one learns one's probable station in life.

Each of these objectives has a constituency, and each takes up a part of the budget and a part of the educational day.

"We Want It All"

Some districts make explicit the nature of the schools as a comprehensive social service agency for youth; in Portland, Maine, for example, each school employs a trained social worker to help students with problems at home. But in most districts, the schools' many social functions are simply taken for granted as part of the system of public

TABLE 4-1

School Goals Preferred by Students, Teachers, and Parents

	Intellectual	Personal	Vocational	Social
Students				
Elementary School	47.1%	17.3%	21.8%	13.8%
Jr. High/Middle School	38.0	18.3	30.3	13.4
High School	27.3	25.6	31.1	15.9
Teachers				
Elementary School	48.9%	33.5%	3.5%	14.0%
Jr. High/Middle School	46.7	29.3	10.1	13.9
High School	45.6	29.7	14.8	9.9
Parents				
Elementary School	57.6%	24.5%	8.6%	9.3%
Jr. High/Middle School	51.1	21.1	18.2	9.5
High School	46.5	19.3	25.5	8.7

Intellectual development: instruction in basic skills in mathematics, reading, written and verbal communication, critical thinking, and problem solving. *Personal development:* instruction that builds self-confidence, creativity, ability to think independently, and self-discipline. *Vocational development:* instruction that prepares students for employment, develops skills necessary for getting a job, and fosters awareness of career alternatives. *Social development:* instruction that helps students learn to get along with other students and adults, prepares students for social and civic effectiveness, and develops students' awareness and appreciation of their own and other cultures.

Source: John I. Goodlad, *A Place Called School: Prospects for the Future* (New York: McGraw-Hill Book Company, 1984).

After rating the four areas on a scale ranging from "very unimportant" to "very important," respondents selected one preferred goal from among the four.

education. The goals the public schools strive to reach are worthy goals, and the services they provide are useful and necessary. The value of inculcating habits of good health or preparing young people for parenthood is not at issue. The questions are these: Given current resources in time and money, can the schools pursue all of these objectives successfully? And, if they cannot, should we limit what we expect of them?

To reach a consensus on a limited number of objectives will not be easy. A study by John I. Goodlad found that parents, teachers, and students expect the schools to serve comprehensive needs. Asked to rate the four broad areas of development that make up a typical curriculum—intellectual, personal, social, and vocational—each group found most of these broad goals "very important." Furthermore, when the respondents were allowed to choose a single preferred goal, only half the teachers and parents agreed upon the same goal. Half the parents and almost half the teachers chose the intellectual category, but the other half of each group distributed this choice of a single goal across the other three categories—personal, social, and vocational. Among students, the absence of agreement was more marked: They spread their preferences widely across all four areas (see Table 4-1). Building a consensus on goals will be difficult if, as Goodlad concludes, "We want it all," and if we also believe the school can give us what we want.

Constituencies as Lobbies

Powerful lobbies have organized around each of the functions assumed by the schools—each fighting for larger shares of school time and budgets. Often, the most vigorous lobbying comes from the newer subject areas such as vocational education and auto-driver training. These subjects, which were introduced into the curriculum after 1920 amid great controversy, have had to rely on state laws in order to gain a secure place in the curriculum. The "standard" subjects such as mathematics and English, which never had to use political power to justify their place in the curriculum, were consequently less frequently mandated by state law until 1983–84. In these two years 34 states established requirements in academic subjects for high school graduation as a reaction to the political pressures for academic excellence discussed in Chapter 2. Associations of teachers of special subjects can be very influential at the state level. Vocational education, physical education, and home economics teachers use their state affiliates of the National Education Association (NEA) to ensure that their specialties are stressed in the local schools. They are supported by manufacturers of hardware, such as sports equipment and home appliances, required by the newer courses. Many high school students were required to take only one year of science or math but four years of physical education. Teachers of driver's education make up a state lobby newer than the others, but they have been so effective that almost all states now mandate this subject.

By contrast, the teachers of academic subjects are usually poorly organized or weakly united at the state level. During the more than seven years I spent on the state board of education, the math or English teachers never requested an opportunity to speak and never lobbied. But the vocational education and physical education teachers pushed for some specific policy every year. A consequence of this lobbying is the large percentage of the curriculum held by vocational education,

TABLE 4-2

**Instructional Time Allotted to Subject Areas
in Selected Junior and Senior High Schools**

Junior High	Percent	Senior High	Percent
English	22	Vocational Education	24
Math	17	English	18
Social Studies	14	Math	13
Science	13	Social Studies	13
Vocational Education	11	Science	11
Arts	11	Physical Education	9
Physical Education	10	Arts	8
Foreign Language	2	Foreign Language	4

Source: John I. Goodlad, *A Place Called School: Prospects for the Future* (New York: McGraw-Hill Book Company, 1984).

as much as 24 percent in some schools (see Table 4-2). The teachers in traditional academic areas like math and social studies relied in large part on college entrance requirements to assure their place in the curriculum. When colleges lowered their academic requirements in the 1970s, these academic subjects lost some of their priority. That the national trend is to require less professional training for teaching licenses in physics, math, or history than for home economics or industrial arts illustrates how little influence the teachers of traditional core subjects wield.

When a constituency is so well organized that it becomes a lobby, it has power. James Koerner summarizes very well the process by which this power is felt:

> Suppose a local board, aware of the obsolescence and flac-cidity of much that passes for vocational training . . . decides to reduce its program . . . In theory this is one of its sovereign rights. In practice several things occur to change its mind. First, the vocational education lobby goes to work on other members of local government and on the state legislature or state department of education to protect the extensive interests of vocational education teachers. Second, the re-gional accrediting association comes to the aid of the status quo and makes threatening noises, suggesting and then perhaps demanding, on pain of disaccreditation . . . that the board rescind its decision. Third, the NEA state affiliate

TABLE 4-3

A Typical School District Budget, 1973

Elementary Education Programs (grades K-6)

Kindergarten	$ 244,320
Grade 1	611,585
Grade 2	554,989
Grade 3	533,070
Grade 4	571,425
Grade 5	561,701
Grade 6	488,893
Title I[a]	132,275
General Education, Elementary	811,013
Total	$ 4,509,271

Secondary Education Programs (grades 7-12)

Agriculture	$ 13,002
Athletics	162,740
Business Education	184,199
Co-Curricular Activities[b]	24,173
Distributive Activities[c]	14,229
Driver Education	127,557
English	726,605
Foreign Languages	278,142
Guidance Services	326,756
Health Instruction	21,816
Home Economics	152,797
Humanities	5,945
Industrial Education	379,374
Mathematics	553,833
Music	5,547
School Newspaper	14,240
School Yearbook	1,441
Science	526,746
Social Sciences	697,082
General Education, Secondary	553,636
Total	$ 4,769,860

Programs Related to Instruction (grades K-12)

Art	$ 313,494
Audio-visual Services	134,949
Health Services	33,856
Instructional Materials Centers	30,443
Instruction & Curriculum Coordination/Supervision	255,018
Intramurals	90,871
Library Services	480,738
Music	497,932
Physical Education	499,318
Planetarium	25,604
Reading	426,269
Resource Centers	212,311
Special Education[d]	622,491
Summer School Instruction	230,675
Total	$ 3,853,969

General Program Areas (grades K-12)

Community and Recreation Services	$ 34,200
Noon Supervision	33,250
Substitute Teachers	135,000
Transportation	640,960
Operation & Maintainence of Plant	2,754,530
Fringe Benefits & Insurance	596,200
Debt Service Fund	2,100,900
Total	$ 6,295,040

Programs at _____ Area Vocational Institute
Vocational Programs for Secondary Students[e]

Pre-vocational Training	$ 42,350
Continuing Education Center	21,750
Subtotal	$ 64,100
Regular Vocational Programs	
Agriculture	$ 21,406
Business & Office Education	151,846
Health Occupations	125,612
Home Economics	48,691
Technical Education	94,724
Trades & Industry	112,954
Vocational Food Training	17,048
Multimedia Resource Center	15,900
Work Study	2,400
General Administration & Services	92,961
Maintainence-Operation of Plant	89,150
Subtotal	$ 772,692
Adult Evening Programs	
Adult Basic Education	$ 14,761
Classes for Persons with Special Needs	34,925
General Adult Education	16,500
Adult Evening Vocational	51,900
Subtotal	$ 118,086
Total	$ 954,878

Districtwide General Support Services

Board of Education	$ 34,600
Superintendent	54,554
Assistant to the Superintendent	35,415
Business Office	179,182
Data Processing	67,600
Personnel Office	53,573
Public Information	13,500
Student Accounting Office	37,000
Total	$ 475,424

Total Budget $20,858,442

[a] Title I provides compensatory education for slow-learning, economically disadvantaged students.
[b] Co-curricular activities are activities in support of an academic program (field trips and the like).
[c] Distributive education generally relates to vocational education.
[d] Special Education is education for the handicapped.
[e] Note that expenses for vocational education appear under two headings, one for vocational courses taught on the school site and one for vocational courses offered at a regional site.

Source: Stephen J. Knezevich, *Program Budgeting* (Berkeley, California: McCutchan Publishing Corporation, 1973), pp. 126-127.

"investigates" and through its considerable power "per-suades" the board to a different view.[3]

Thus the multiple objectives aimed at by the schools have strong support in outside agencies—state legislatures, professional associations, lobbies, and accrediting associations—as well as colleges and universities.

The national reports published in 1983 criticized this lack of balance between academic and non-academic courses. (See Table 4-3 to compare expenditures on academic and non-academic portions of the curriculum in a typical midwestern school district. Note that expenditures for vocational education appear under two headings, one for vocational courses maintained at the school site and one for vocational courses offered at a regional site.) The reform movements of the 1980s have been a reaction to the lack of lobbying power exercised on behalf of the academic subjects.

Constituencies, Crises, and Curriculum

The inability of educational policy to satisfy all the schools' constituencies sets in motion the pendulum swings that are a central feature of "crises" in education. Disaffected constituents who want more art or football are also property owners and taxpayers. Among the several causes of the tax revolts of the late seventies was dissatisfaction over the performance of the public schools. Frequently, school boards react by adding new functions to the schools without eliminating any of the old. Such a policy of addition results in public schools like the comprehensive suburban high school in Highland Park, Illinois, which offered 252 discrete courses.[4] The senior high school manual of Salt Lake City lists 350 separate courses, offered at various of its nine high schools, which serve a student population of 60,000. This district (the Granite School District, of which Terrel H. Bell was superintendent before his appointment as Secretary of Education by President Reagan) has specific requirements for its various categories of students. In some districts, however, one consequence of too great a breadth of choice is that students who would like to go on to college often have failed to take the required solid subjects in their senior year. (See the typical high school curriculum of 1893, Table 4-4; excerpts from course catalogues at comprehensive high schools, 1978-82, Tables 4-5 and 4-6; and representative students' schedules current in California Table 4-7.)

TABLE 4-4

High School Curriculum for 1893
with Recommended Number of Periods per Week

1ST SECONDARY SCHOOL YEAR	2ND SECONDARY SCHOOL YEAR

Latin . . . . 5 p.
English Literature, 2 p. ⎫
English Composition, 2 p. ⎬ . . . . . . 4 p.
German [or French] . . . . 5 p.
History of Italy, Spain, & France . . . 3 p.
Applied Geography (European
    political; continental &
    oceanic flora & fauna) . . . . 4 p.
<div align="right">25 p.</div>
	Latin . . . . 4 p.
	Greek . . . . 5 p.
	English Literature, 2 p. ⎫
	English Composition, 2 p. ⎬ . . . . . . 4 p.
	German [continued] . . . . 4 p.
	French [begun] . . . . 5 p.
	Algebra [or Bookkeeping &
	    Commercial Arithmetic], 2 p. ⎫ . . .4p.
	Geometry, 2 p. ⎬
	Botany or Zoology . . . . 4 p.
	English History to 1688 . . . . 3 p.
	<div align="right">33 p.</div>

3RD SECONDARY SCHOOL YEAR	4TH SECONDARY SCHOOL YEAR

Latin . . . . 4 p.
Greek . . . . 4 p.
English Literature, 2 p. ⎫
English Composition, 1 p. ⎬ . . . . . . 4 p.
Rhetoric, 1 p. ⎭
German . . . . 4 p.
French . . . . 4 p.
Algebra [or Bookkeeping &
    Commercial Arithmetic], 2 p. ⎫ . . . 4p.
Geometry, 2 p. ⎬
Physics . . . . 4 p.
History, English and American . . . . 3 p.
Astronomy, 3 p. 1st ½ yr. ⎫
Meteorology, 3 p. 2nd ½ yr. ⎬ . . . . . . 3 p.
<div align="right">34 p.</div>
	Latin . . . . 4 p.
	Greek . . . . 4 p.
	English Literature, 2 p. ⎫
	English Composition, 1 p. ⎬ . . . . . . 4 p.
	English Grammar, 1 p. ⎭
	German . . . . 4 p.
	French . . . . 4 p.
	Trigonometry ⎫
	Higher Algebra ⎬ . . . . 2 p.
	Chemistry . . . . 4 p.
	History [intensive] &
	    Civil Government . . . . 3 p.
	Geology or Physiography,
	    4 p. 1st ½ yr. ⎫
	Anatomy, Physiology, & ⎬ . . . . . . 4 p.
	    Hygiene, 4 p. 2nd ½ yr. ⎭
	<div align="right">33 p.</div>

Curriculum as of 1893 preferred by the Committee of Ten; it became the standard for all public high schools.

Conflicts in Values Again

Broadly speaking, the constituencies that influence education policy cluster around basic values—chiefly, pragmatic efficiency, egalitarianism, and individualism, or freedom of choice.

Schemes to produce school efficiency have been introduced throughout our history, and efficiency is a highly regarded value at the moment. Advocates of efficiency, now as around the turn of the century, may see central control as a means to that end. If the public so decides, we could have a statewide curriculum and testing program. But central

TABLE 4-5

Selected Senior High School Course Offerings
Berkeley School District, California

Home Economics and Family Life Department

Social Living: Social Living is a required nine-week course designed to give students an opportunity to learn facts and to share with each other their ideas and concerns about social issues and problems that affect them. The basic subject matter includes sexuality, drug abuse, V.D., pregnancy, birth, death, understanding personality, life-styles, ethnic awareness, personal values, and interpersonal relationships. Each class is unique due to the varied backgrounds and experiences of all Berkeley High School sophomores. The teacher facilitates learning through lectures, discussions and by presenting speakers and films. Activities will be provided to develop students' skills in communication and problem solving.

Wide World Foods: This class is intended for students who are interested in cooking as a hobby or a profession. Basic cooking techniques, nutrition, meal planning are taught against a background of foods from other countries. Cooking from countries on every continent is covered: Demonstrations, lectures, films, and student preparation of food from each country.

Lunch Bunch Service: The students will run a lunch service for staff in B144; on clear days, patio dining. The service will resemble the sandwich shops which have become popular in Berkeley. The purpose of the class will be to acquaint students with a work experience, one that is available in our community. Students will prepare the food, manage the money exchange and costs, and serve the "public." The class will cover the following areas: public health rules for food handlers, cooperation with other workers, responsibility and proper behavior in a work situation, using a cash register and accounting for money exchange.

Design Department

Crafts Workshop: Personal and home arts and crafts are explored. Example of crafts to learn: needlepoint embroidery, Italian quilting, macrame, crocheting, quilting.

Performing Arts Department

Journalism-Radio Broadcasting: The course is intended to train students in all phases of radio production, including hand signals, news casting, sport reporting, morning shows, "DJ" operation, interviews, talk shows, on-the-spot reporting, production of commercials, and other types of programs, methods and techniques related to radio. Guest speakers, demonstrations, and various field trips will be made to radio and television stations, other high schools with radio production setups, and other places that relate to broadcasting, to further enhance the student's exposure to radio as it is today. Fulfills English elective graduation requirements.

Business Education Department

Office Machines: Students will learn touch operation of electric ten-key and electronic calculating machines. In addition, they will learn efficient operation of transcription equipment which is used in place of shorthand in some offices. A short filing course and proper usage of the telephone will also be covered. Duplicating machines will be introduced for those who have had little or no instruction in this area. This class is strongly recommended for students planning to work in an office.

Model Office: Model Office is a course designed for students who have taken a number of business courses and who would like to use their knowledge and skills in a real office situation. The class is set up as an office for a particular company, and the students are employees of that company. Available positions include an office manager, department managers, account clerks, payroll clerk, typists, file clerks, secretaries, etc. The duties performed are similar to the duties performed in a real office and should meet business office standards.

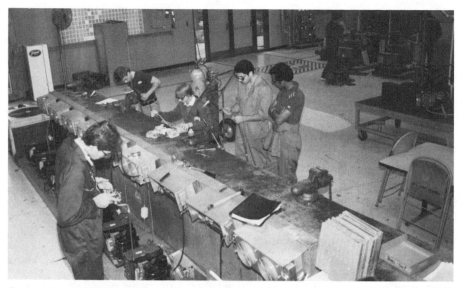

Courses in vocational education take up 11 percent of instructional time in some junior high (or middle) schools and 24 percent of instructional time in some secondary schools.

control, whether by states or by the federal government, conflicts with another deeply held value—and a value recently in the ascendancy—freedom of choice, a value manifested in local control of education by 16,000 thousand separate school boards.

Neither efficiency nor freedom of choice, however, is a more deeply ingrained value than egalitarianism. Equal educational opportunity may be viewed as assurance of equal access to education, or as equal treatment of students, or as equal educational outcomes. Equal access is illustrated by the state's guarantee of a minimally acceptable level of local school services. Federal antidiscrimination and desegregation laws are also essential to the application of this concept. For some students, equal access is not enough; they need special programs. Equal treatment may be seen as the state's recognition that learners have widely varying characteristics and abilities—that specific resources are required for specific circumstances and for particular students. Equality conceived of as similar outcomes in student achievement became a political principle in 1970. This result could be measured by scores on achievement tests, and proponents of this view contended that the school rather than the pupil should be held responsible for substandard attainment.

TABLE 4-6

Selected Senior High School Course Offerings
Granite School District, Utah

Home Economics Education

Foods 2: Students who enjoy cooking and desire to develop food-related skills should include this class in their schedules. Attention will be given to meal preparation with emphasis on marketing, budgeting, good nutrition and cooking skills. Seasonable food preparation will provide experiences related to family foods, meals for entertaining and special holidays, foreign foods and creative foods. Experience with a variety of cookware, appliances and serving styles will be provided. Under-weight and over-weight problems and special diets will be studied.

Housing and Interior Design: Effort and money are required in order to provide a satisfactory home. This class will help students to understand housing needs and costs. Units of study include evaluation of floor plans, needs vs. wants, renting vs. buying, storage centers, color schemes, floor and window treatments, furnishings, equipment and methods of payment including interest costs. A study of city and county building laws is included. This class would be of special interest to a career-bound architect or to a creative student with an interest in design.

Independent Living: Following graduation from high school some young people leave their family home for employment, education, or other experiences. They find themselves, for the first time, fully responsible for their own well being. This course consists of a variety of short units related to selection and maintenance of clothing, apartment living, food selection, health care, purchasing and preparing food, money management, and living on a budget.

Industrial Education

Jewelry Making: This course is designed for students who are interested in employment in the jewelry manufacturing industry. Instruction is given in the design, fabrication, and repair of all types of jewelry. Students receive practical experience working with gold, silver, natural and synthetic stones, and other materials used in the manufacture and repair of jewelry.

Tile Setting and Plastering: This course is designed for the student who plans to become either a tile setter, plasterer or dry wall applicator. The learning experiences include the installation and finishing of wall board, plaster board, tile, and other interior wall surfaces.

Upholstery: This is a vocational course about the materials, tools, and equipment needed to construct or recondition upholstered furniture. Students will develop job-entry skills in attaching webbing, sewing and attaching springs, positioning and anchoring stuffing materials, and using foam rubber.

Meat Cutting: This course is designed for the students whose vocational goal is to become a meat cutter. Specialized classroom and practical experiences are gained by the cutting, trimming, and preparation of different kinds of meats and poultry. Students who achieve job-entry level skills may be placed at a store for on-the-job training.

But freedom of choice conflicts with efficiency and equality. Local boards complain when they must cut back on programs preferred by local residents, such as programs in music and the arts, in order to cover the cost of federal or state mandates for handicapped and bilingual children. Local boards (all 16,000 of them) have the power to choose segregated schools, or inadequate funding for the handicapped, or high-cost instructional techniques, or inefficient managerial policies. Or they can reject statewide minimum competency objectives in reading and math.

In short, these three values—egalitarianism, pragmatic efficiency, and freedom of choice (or individualism)—cannot all be maximized at the same time. Education policy alternates among these competing values as our national mood shifts toward equity (1964-70) or freedom of choice (1969-74) or efficiency (1978-81). Conflicts centering on these competing values are likely to become even more intense as the 1980s progress. The federal government in the early eighties has been willing to ease up on its demands for equality and to permit wider local (and state) choice. The proposal by the Reagan administration to prune the regulations from federal categorical programs for the handicapped and disadvantaged is a definite tilt toward free (local) choice. In addition, the fiscal stress in states such as Michigan will bring about an intensified search for efficient policies—for example, the closing of low-enrollment schools. In California, Proposition 13, by limiting the amount of property tax, the traditional source of school funding, caused school districts to charge fees for participation in school athletics, thereby restricting equality of access to sports programs, as poor families may not be able to pay the required fees.

Moreover, the 1983-85 demand for "excellence" is tending to push all three of the prior competing values into the background. Some of the policies meant to achieve excellence, such as statewide achievement tests and graduation standards, may prove inefficient and inegalitarian. They may too greatly restrict local school boards in responding to local conditions and, indirectly, cause disadvantaged students to drop out. During the eighties we will need to choose among competing values, to decide where to place the greatest weight and emphasis.

A Success Story—Title I

Conflicts in values, fortunately, do yield to resolution and the establishment of consensus. There have been times when a national consensus in support of education policy allowed the school system

TABLE 4-7

**Representative Programs of Study for High School Students
(11th Grade, California)**

General Track Courses	Units	Subject
Language Skills	10	English
Advanced Glee	10	Music
Cafeteria Aide	10	Work Experience
Junior Physical Education	10	Physical Education
Basic U.S. History	7.5	Social Studies
Advanced Foods	5	Home Economics
Beginning Arts and Crafts	5	Art
Introductory Life Sciences	2.5	Science
Exploring Childhood	2.5	Home Economics

Vocational Track Courses	Units	Subject
Work Experience	20	Work Experience
American Literature, Advanced Grammar	10	English
Agricultural Business, Feeds and Feeding	10	Agriculture
Junior Physical Education	10	Physical Education
U.S. History	5	Social Studies
Math Today	2.5	Math

College Preparatory Track Courses	Units	Subject
Algebra 2	10	Math
English Literature, Advanced Grammar	10	English
Chemistry	10	Science
U.S. History	10	Social Studies
Spanish 3	10	Foreign Language
Junior Physical Education	10	Physical Education

Source: Report prepared for California State Department of Education, *California Curriculum Study: Paths through High School* (1984). Appendix B report, prepared by Nancy Sanders and Nancy Stone.

With information gathered from secondary schools throughout the state, a study of schools in California has constructed three typical patterns of study. Upon graduating, the "general track" and "vocational track" students may attend a community college or a state college; the "college preparatory track" student may attend a state university or a selective private college. For a typical student, the junior year represents a significant investment of energy in academic subjects. The senior year is usually marked by fewer core academic courses.

to accomplish extraordinary goals. The establishment of common schools made America the first nation to aspire to universal free education through 12 grades. More recently, consensus on the value of egalitarianism, expressed through some of the programs of President Johnson's War on Poverty, have illustrated what public education can accomplish.

Title I of the federal Elementary and Secondary Education Act (1965) provided compensatory education programs directed toward low achievers among the disadvantaged urban and rural populations. These programs were a success. A high percentage of the disadvantaged urban population is black, and the academic performance of low-achieving black students in elementary grades, a group targeted by the Title I programs, has improved (see Tables 4-8 and 4-9). In 1977-78 and 1979-80, students from all levels of the school system—elementary, middle, and high school—were tested in reading and mathematics. The scores were compared with scores earned five years before in the same subjects. This national assessment showed that black students at the low end of the achievement band had, at the elementary and junior high levels of the school system, substantially improved their performance in mathematics and reading. In the elementary school group, tested at age 9, low achievers had improved by 5 percentage points. During the same period (between 1964 and 1976), colleges accelerated aid and outreach programs for promising black students. The same national assessment of reading and mathematics showed that high-achieving black students (both elementary and secondary) had also improved their scores, in part, perhaps, motivated by the opportunity to attend college.

Results, recently released, of the largest study ever undertaken of elementary education, the Sustaining Effects Study directed by Launor F. Carter, document even more fully the success of the Title I programs in compensatory education. Portions of Carter's summary of these results appear on page 68. The improvement in the academic skills and achievement of black students, especially those in urban schools, in the last decade shows in a most encouraging way that when we have a clear policy objective and stick to it, we can improve the performance of our schools.

The success of the schools in the next decade will depend upon how we set priorities and how fixedly we focus upon our central objectives. If we are to improve the schools' performance, we will need to make hard choices among the multiple functions they have been assigned. At the same time we must avoid overcorrection of the system; we must not move too far in the direction of setting uniform standards of academic performance. Very few of the new state and local requirements are augmented by the introduction of methods to motivate students to study more math or science—except, of course,

TABLE 4-8

Reading Achievement for 9-, 13-, and 17-Year-Olds, 1971-80

| | Mean Percent Correct | Mean Change | |
	1979-80	From 1974-75 to 1979-80	From 1971-72 to 1974-75
9-Year-Olds			
Average	67.9%	2.6%	2.4%
Male	66.0	3.0	1.4
Female	69.7	2.3	1.0
White	69.3	2.3	4.8
Hispanic	60.3	5.3	NA*
Black	59.6	5.1	1.2
13-Year-Olds			
Average	60.8%	0.9%	0.1%
Male	58.8	1.2	0.1
Female	62.6	0.4	0.2
White	62.6	0.7	0.8
Hispanic	51.5	2.5	NA
Black	49.6	3.2	0.3
17-Year-Olds			
Average	68.2%	−0.8%	−0.1%
Male	66.9	−0.4	−0.1
Female	69.7	−1.0	−0.1
White	70.6	−0.6	0.4
Hispanic	58.8	2.0	NA
Black	52.2	0.1	0.2

*Not available.

Sources: Department of Education, National Center for Education Statistics, *Digest of Education Statistics* (Washington, D.C.: U.S. Government Printing Office, 1980, 1982); National Assessment of Education Progress, *Three National Assessments of Reading: Changes in Performance* (Denver, Colorado: National Assessment of Education Progress, 1979-80, 1981).

Title I of the Elementary and Secondary Education Act (1965) provided funds for compensatory education programs in elementary and junior high grades, directed toward low-achieving students among the disadvantaged urban and rural populations. Between 1971-72 and 1979-80 students in this category improved their performance in reading and mathematics.

for the withholding of a diploma. Subject matter needs to be made more interesting as well as more demanding.

A broad curriculum choice for students was adopted in the hope that it would, by making school more interesting to students, enhance school retention. The overcorrection of 1983 has run in the direction of state or local mandates that specify numbers of years to be spent in the study of academic subjects. In some localities, high school students have had a great deal of choice at one time (between 1968

TABLE 4-9

Mathematics Achievement for 9-, 13-, and 17-Year Olds, 1972-78

	Mean Percent Correct	Mean Change
	1977-78	From 1972-73 to 1977-78
9-Year-Olds		
Average	36.8%	−1.3%
Male	37.0	−1.2
Female	36.7	−1.4
White	39.1	−2.0
Hispanic	28.6	0.6
Black	26.3	2.9
13-Year-Olds		
Average	50.6%	−2.0%
Male	50.9	−1.8
Female	50.2	−2.3
White	54.2	−2.4
Hispanic	36.7	−3.0
Black	32.4	0.6
17-Year-Olds		
Average	48.1%	−3.6%
Male	49.9	−3.9
Female	46.4	−3.2
White	51.0	−3.5
Hispanic	36.0	−2.3
Black	30.9	−2.6

Source: Department of Education, National Center for Education Statistics, *Digest of Education Statistics* (Washington, D.C.: U.S. Government Printing Office, 1980, 1982).

and 1972) and almost none at another (1984). Rather than seesawing between one goal and another, we need to forge a consensus on a core curriculum that can be taught in stimulating ways and to build an elective structure on top of this core.

Limiting Goals and Expectations

We must think in terms of trade-offs to achieve balance and emphasis as we reduce and define our schools' goals. If we want to put more emphasis upon academic skills, especially skills in science and mathematics, we shall have to make a choice: We can give up some of our current aims—or we can extend the school day or year. A 1984 Gallup poll, however, reveals that a majority of the American public does not favor a longer school day or year. The nine-and-one-half-month school year seems deeply ingrained in American culture.

Compensatory Education[4]

The Sustaining Effects Study was started in 1975. Data were collected on as many as 120,000 students in a representative sample of over 300 elementary schools throughout the country for 3 successive school years, starting with the 1976–77 school year.

Title I students received:

- Services costing about $436 more than the services regular students received. Most of this money was spent on teachers, remedial specialists, and aides.
- Considerably more hours of instruction in reading and math than did regular students.
- Less of their instruction in large groups in regular classrooms and more instruction in small-group settings from special teachers and aides.

Many individuals have questioned the effectiveness of Compensatory Education. Indeed, this has been a concern of Congress, as was shown when the Elementary and Secondary Education Act was passed in 1965. The Act's Title I program was conceived as part of the "War on Poverty," and one of its major justifications was the desire to improve the educational opportunities of the poor and educationally disadvantaged. Funds were made available to all states and in turn to local school districts to support additional instruction at schools in economically poorer areas. Funding soon reached over a billion dollars a year, and since 1965 more than $40 billion has been spent for Title I activities. In view of the large sums involved and the concern of some members of Congress that the local school districts might not use the money as intended, the Act required that the Title I program be evaluated.

The results reported here represent the largest and most comprehensive evaluation of the effectiveness of Title I ever undertaken.

For each grade, results are based on about 1,100 to 3,000 Title I students, about 1,300 to 2,000 needy students, and about 1,700 to 2,500 regular students. (Title I students were reported by their school to be receiving some Title I services, needy students were reported by their teachers as being in need of Title I but not receiving any, and regular students were reported as not needing Title I services and not receiving them.) Statistical analysis showed significant gains for Title I students, relative to needy students, for the mathematics section of the Comprehensive Tests of Basic Skills. This was true for grades 1 through 6. For the reading section of the Comprehensive Tests of Basic Skills, significant reading gains were found for grades 1 through 3, but not for grades 4, 5, or 6. The largest relative gains are in the first grade, and this is also the case for the reading comparisons. The rate of gain for Title I students is at least equal to that of regular students, whereas the rate of gain for needy students who did not receive Title I is not as great as that of either Title I students or regular students.

——Launor F. Carter

Children work together on a writing project in Berkeley, California. Between 1965 and 1975, innovative programs in many places succeeded in heightening the egalitarian atmosphere of the school.

To make the necessary changes would alter the contour and scope of the school curriculum, especially the secondary school. For example, guidance and training in specific job skills could be provided at community colleges or in the workplace. (See the courses in job skills listed in Tables 4-5 and 4-6.) This would consign to the secondary schools only the minor role of developing in students an awareness of the variety of careers and kinds of work. Similarly, we could spin off from the schools their function as purveyors of information about health and nutrition. Physical education, now in many districts a required subject that consumes 45 minutes of each day and demands the employment of thousands of teachers across the country, could become voluntary throughout the secondary grades. Such changes— no more shop, no more team sports for most adolescents—may seem shocking. But changes of this magnitude are what we must project— and implement—if we are to bring school performance and public expectations into balance.

Setting priorities and limiting objectives need not be seen as a matter of cutting out functions only. We can focus the curriculum of the schools more carefully. Right now, for example, social studies (including history) is a confused and much too diffuse area, featuring everything from psychology to anthropology. We need to decide what knowledge contributes most to citizenship and then develop a unified, sequential program of social studies to convey that knowledge. Perhaps history should be assigned the top priority and social science left largely to postsecondary education. If the public can agree on the knowledge and skills that are appropriate and essential, we can develop a common core curriculum, with sequence, scope, and integration across grades and levels of skill, a curriculum with an element and strand for all pupils regardless of the high school tracks they pursue. Secondary school students could still have some electives on top of this common core curriculum.

By setting priorities, discarding some objectives, and focusing more carefully upon the objectives we retain, we can improve the match between public expectations about performance and the school performance the public perceives. To make such changes, however, will be to face some of the political obstacles and contradictions inherent in our school system. Some of the special lobbies will have to lose out and receive lower priority. To lower societal expectations for the schools will require coalition building unlike any that we have experienced in recent years. Vocational and physical educators along with social scientists will be unhappy.

Reducing the number of objectives our schools face is not the only way to proceed. We could change the quantity of resources we allot to education. The Japanese pupils, who attend school about 240 days a year, do not take the vacations that limit our school year to 178 days. We could follow their example. Or, we could more efficiently automate our school system through computers, as we have certain of our industries. Of course, either solution to our problems would be costly. Expanding the school year by 20 percent would cost 20 billion dollars. And while computer automation could substitute capital equipment for teachers, it is unlikely that teachers' unions will permit this to happen. Even if they do, computers will probably supplement rather than supplant a human being in the classroom.

If we wish to give our schools in the next decades much the same resources we have given them in the past, and at the same time to improve their performance, then we need to sort out their objectives and to focus on those that can be met in a way that will satisfy our reasonable expectations. Otherwise, the pendulum will continue its drastic swings, as the schools focus now on some, now on others, of their multiple objectives, and alienate neglected constituencies.

CHAPTER

HOW WELL DO OUR SCHOOLS PERFORM?

Our educational system, rooted as it is in our history and our structure of values, has often been a source of justifiable pride. Whatever its limitations, the public education system of the United States (including higher education) is the most egalitarian system in the world.

Thomas Jefferson had counted on education to develop only that "natural aristocracy" of the few whose talents justly deserved to be developed for the benefit of society. But Horace Mann and the common school advocates wanted universal education; to them, education was to be the "balance wheel" of society. Mann proclaimed in 1848:

> If one class possesses all the wealth and education, while the residue of society is ignorant and poor, it matters not by what name the relation between them may be called; the latter, in fact, and in truth, will be the servile dependents and subjects of the former. But if education be equally diffused, it will draw property after it, by the strongest of all attractions; for such a thing never did happen, as that an intelligent and practical body of men should be permanently poor. Education, then, beyond all other devices of human origin, is the great equalizer of the conditions of men, the balance wheel of the social machinery.[1]

The public schools were thought of by their supporters as a secure system for moderating pernicious social inequalities.

The egalitarianism of the American system distinguishes it from the school systems of the European democracies. About 75 percent of our students graduate from high school, and some 44 percent go on to higher education. In most other Western nations, students are diverted into vocational and technical programs at age 14 or 15, and only 15 to 30 percent are graduated from a secondary school. Considering the large percentage of teenagers the U.S. schools enroll, the level of attainment of these students is surprisingly high.

Our school system has grown steadily more egalitarian. As recently as 1940, fewer than 50 percent of the pupils in this country completed high school. By 1984, 75 percent did. Conscious and determined effort over the last 20 years has increased access to higher education among those least represented in the past—the minority groups. While college enrollment of white students grew slightly, the proportion of Blacks in college more than doubled in the same period, growing between 1965 and 1976 from 5 to 11 percent. In 1981 the percentage of black high school graduates who went on to college *exceeded* that of whites for the first time. That many of these students come from lower socioeconomic groups makes this achievement all the more remarkable. Recent sociological studies from the Soviet Union, by contrast, indicate that an unexpectedly high share of the places in most of its elite postsecondary institutions go to children of white-collar workers.

Lately, however, the headlines have warned us that our schools are not competitive with those of our economic rivals West Germany and Japan, and that current graduates of our secondary schools cannot match the records set by their predecessors as recently as 1970. Now, when the performance of our schools is a source of widespread dissatisfaction, we need to consider carefully how we measure that performance.

Comparing Apples and Oranges

One way to measure performance is to test "outcomes"—the skills or knowledge gained by students—and to compare what students learn in the United States with what students at the same level learn in West Germany or Japan. The openness of the American system, however—its power to retain students up to the age of 17 or 18—makes it difficult to draw valid comparisons of outcomes between this and other systems. As Table 5-1 shows, the U.S. ranks first in percentage of 15- to 24-year-olds enrolled in school.

Torsten Husén, professor in the Institute of International Education at the University of Stockholm and an expert in the international assessment of school performance, explains why international com-

TABLE 5-1

Enrollment Rates for Students Aged 15–18 and 20–24

Country		Age 15–18			Age 20–24	
	Year	*Percent Enrolled*	*Ranking*	Year	*Percent Enrolled*	*Ranking*
Austria	1969	31.9%	14	1972	14.8%	12
Belgium	1966	54.2	7	1971	20.5	6
Canada	1970	78.1	2	1970	28.5	2
Denmark	1970	51.7	9	1972	23.7	3
Finland	1967	47.4	10	1972	13.8	13
France	1970	54.3	6	1972	17.0	10
Germany (FDR)	1969	30.5	16	1972	17.1	9
Ireland	1971	47.0	11	1970	12.2	14
Italy	1966	30.8	15	1972	20.1	7
Luxembourg	1970	37.4	13	1972	1.9	16
Netherlands	1970	52.5	8	1971	21.2	5
Norway	1970	68.9	3	1972	19.0	8
Sweden	1972	68.1	4	1972	22.4	4
Switzerland	1970	62.6	5	1972	10.3	15
United Kingdom	1970	39.4	12	1972	15.0	11
United States	1970	82.9	1	1972	51.5	1

Source: Rates for 15- to 18-year-olds adapted from UNESCO (1974, Tables 15 and 16); rates for 20- to 24-year-olds adapted from UNESCO (1975, Table 3-2).

The United States enrolls a higher percentage of young people in secondary school and college than does any other Western nation.

parisons do not accurately assess the performance of the U.S. school system. All comparisons must begin from a base of similarity, or they fail, as in the proverbial comparison of apples and oranges. The differences between American and European schools are so great that a base of comparison is nearly impossible to establish. Even general terms like "primary" and "secondary" education undergo transformation when they cross national boundaries.

European primary and secondary schools differ from those in the United States in governance, purpose, and enrollment. In West Germany, for instance, both primary and secondary schools are under the control of a central state or *land* government (like Bavaria). Primary schools are at least partially funded by the government, and secondary schools are wholly so. All German schools are inspected by representatives of a central agency, usually a state ministry of education. At the level of the secondary school, the difference in purpose is even more striking to an American than the difference in governance. European secondary schools have traditionally existed for students who from their earliest years attend private rather than public institutions, and these public secondary schools still exist to educate an elite and to train them for entrance to the universities. In England and Germany, the last year of secondary school includes those who in the United States would be in the college freshman age group.

The attack on the elitism of the European systems during the 1960s had its effects: students are no longer tracked as early or as consistently as they previously were, although by our standards European secondary schools are still elitist. Before the 1960s, students entering academic secondary schools transferred into them from grade 4 or 5 of primary school. Secondary school occupied six to nine years and covered a curriculum geared to requirements set by the universities. In the 1950s, only 5 to 10 percent of the pupils in Western and Northern Europe completed academic secondary school and took the "school-leaving" examination that also served as an entrance examination to the universities. From the mid-fifties to the early seventies, enrollment in European secondary schools greatly increased but still included only about 20 percent of the relevant age group. In some countries, the percentage was even less. In the mid-sixties, when 75 percent of the pupils who had entered the system in the first grade were graduated from secondary school in the United States, only 9 percent were graduated in West Germany.

U.S. versus West German Schools

To compare American schools with West German schools, then, is to compare a comprehensive system with an elite system. At no point are the two similar enough to bear comparison. To compare secondary school achievement in Germany and in the United States would be to measure a university-bound group in Germany against a general youth population in the United States. Even if one compared the university-bound groups in the two countries, a base of comparison would be lacking. In Germany, the university-bound group represents a much smaller percentage of the youth population than the corresponding group in the United States, and its members have been selected much earlier.

Furthermore, the curriculum of the two systems varies greatly. In the United States, even the elite group—in terms of academic achievement—has been prepared in a comprehensive curriculum. A large portion of their time in school has been spent in the study of subjects for which there is no parallel in West German schools. There is no large vocational track in European secondary schools; vocational training is normally conducted at the employer's workplace. Nor do students study health or physical education or crafts. When I visited West Germany, I was struck with the brevity of their school day—about 8:00 A.M. to 12:30 P.M. Because homework is assigned a much higher priority, school hours do not need to be as long as ours, and all extracurricular activities are conducted by community agencies rather than by the schools.

Comparing Elite and Comprehensive Systems

When basic differences in structure and enrollment between our schools and those of other industrialized countries are taken into account, we see that our schools are performing better than the headlines would lead us to believe. Our high school graduates score higher on international assessment tests in reading than graduates in all but three other Western industrial nations, despite the fact that those countries graduate a much smaller percentage of their students. When adjustments are made for the great difference in the percentage of young people tested, our students also compare favorably in mathematics and science (see Figures 5-1 and 5-2).

Husén explains how to adjust for these differences: Compare only the small percentage at the top level of the achievement band. Each system presumably retains the most able students, but while selective systems retain *only* those, comprehensive systems retain them as an elite within a larger group. Given that selective systems value most highly the quality of the end product—the elite—to compare the elite of a comprehensive system with the end product of a selective system is fair to both systems.

To illustrate: In the United States, high school seniors include about 75 percent of 17- to 18-year-olds. In Sweden, students who finish grades 10 to 12 (*gymnasium*) make up about 50 percent of the 17- to 18-year-old age group. In the Federal Republic of Germany, grade 13 (*oberprimaner*) accounts for only about 15 percent of the same age group. When tests compared the average performance of students in the terminal grade studying mathematics (see Table 5-1), American high school seniors placed far below "seniors" in other countries. But in the United States, 18 percent of 17- to 18-year-olds took mathematics as against 4 to 5 percent in some European countries. To make a more accurate comparative assessment, the testers took this smallest percentage as a base. When the comparison was based on the average

FIGURE 5-1
**An International Comparison of Test Scores in Mathematics
of Students in Last Year of Secondary School**

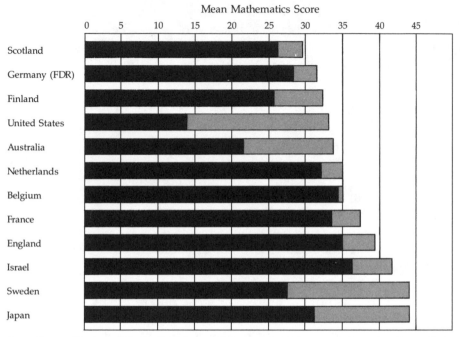

Source: Torsten Husén, ed., *International Study of Achievement in Mathematics: A Comparison Between Twelve Countries* (New York: Wiley, 1967).

▨ Average Mathematics Test Score for Equal Proportion of Age Groups
■ Average Mathematics Test Score for Country

When scores of all students studying mathematics in the terminal year of secondary school are compared, the United States ranks last, in part because U.S. schools enroll a much higher percentage of the relevant age group in mathematics (18 percent as against 5 percent in some European countries). When scores of equal proportions of the age group are compared, U.S. students perform about as well as students in Australia, Belgium, and West Germany.

performance of the top 4 percent of the relevant age group across all participating countries, the range of scores was much narrower (see Figures 5-1 and 5-2). Husén concludes,

> the international surveys of both mathematics and science demonstrated that the top 5 percent to 10 percent at the end of secondary education (i.e., the elite) tended to perform at nearly the same level in both comprehensive and selective systems of secondary education. Thus the elite among U.S.

FIGURE 5-2

**An International Comparison of Test Scores in Science
of Students in Last Year of Secondary School**

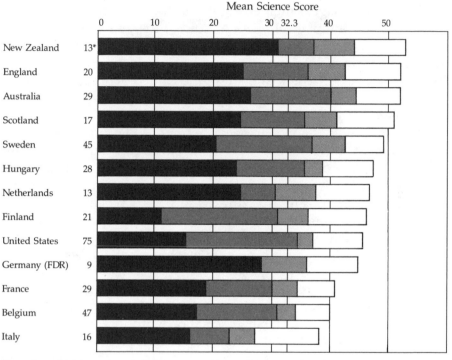

Mean Science Score

*Percentage of total age group tested.

Source: L. C. Comber and John P. Keeves, *Science Education in Nineteen Countries* (Stockholm and New York: Almquist and Wiksell and Wiley-Halsted Press, 1973).

■ Overall Score　■ Top 9%　■ Top 5%　□ Top 1%

International comparisons involving the United States are skewed by the egalitarianism of the U.S. system. When scores compared are adjusted to reflect comparable proportions of the relevant age group, U.S. scores are similar to those of other countries.

high school seniors did not differ considerably in their performance from their age-mates in France, England, or Germany. The comprehensive systems, where the net is cast more widely, result in a bigger 'talent catch.' In addition, those who are less able get a better opportunity to develop their potential than in the selective systems of the traditional European type.[2]

Surveys of international achievement teach another useful lesson: Opportunity to learn is the single factor that best explains differences in performance among students of different countries. A study of French as a foreign language compared eight countries in terms of time spent on the subject (number of years of study); the grade level at which French was introduced in school; and the number of periods of instruction per week. Romania, which requires students to study French for about six years, scored at the top; the United States, which rarely requires French and when it does, requires two years of study at the most, scored at the bottom.

Husén also calls attention to negative trends in European education and documents waves of criticism. Some critics complain of low standards and lack of discipline, while others accuse the schools of being joyless, oppressive, and autocratic. In Europe, as in this country, national commissions are criticizing the secondary schools. There, too, educational institutions have been accused of failing to meet their own goals or society's needs. In the Netherlands and in the Federal Republic of Germany, as in this country, studies show that as they progress through the compulsory schooling grades, from ages 5 through 14, many students become increasingly negative about school. Similarly, too, in the 1960s, when expenditures for education across the Western world grew twice as fast as the gross national product, demands were raised for accountability and tighter public control. Then, during the 1970s, in Germany, Great Britain, and Australia, as in the United States, education slipped down the scale of national priorities, budget growth rates slowed down, and school people practiced the "management of decline." As Table 5-2 demonstrates, the U.S. effort in public school expenditures compares favorably with other nations'.

U.S. versus Japanese Schools

If the comprehensive nature of our school system makes comparison between U.S. students and West German students difficult, there is another country, Japan, where the elementary/secondary schools are at least as egalitarian as our own. (The United States, however, still provides more opportunity for students to acquire a postsecondary education.) In Japan, some 90 percent of all children graduate from the twelfth grade. Furthermore, the Japanese schools have raised the whole base of their youth to a higher level of understanding in mathematics and science. All Japan's high school graduates must complete at least two years of math and two years of science, whereas U.S.

TABLE 5-2

An International Comparison of Expenditures for Public Schools

Country	Year	Expenditure (in millions)	Percent of GNP	Percent of Total Public Expenditure
Sweden	1978	7,850	9.1	13.1
Canada	1978	16,153	8.1	18.5
Saudi Arabia	1979	4,841	7.4	10.2
Soviet Union	1978	47,431	7.4	12.0
Australia	1977	6,402	6.5	16.2
United Kingdom	1976	14,177	6.3	14.3
United States	1977	120,700	6.3	17.7
Austria	1978	3,280	5.7	8.0
Japan	1978	55,563	5.7	16.1
Brazil	1979	1,043	5.6	(NA)
France	1978	25,301	5.3	(NA)
Mexico	1979	6,103	5.2	(NA)
Zaire	1979	363	5.0	25.8
Germany (FDR)	1979	34,699	4.6	(NA)
India	1977	2,923	2.9	9.9
Columbia	1978	513	2.3	19.9

Source: U.S. Bureau of Census, *Statistical Abstract of the United States*, 1983.

U.S. expenditures for public education compare favorably with those of other countries.

school districts typically require only one year of each. College-bound Japanese students study math every year in high school and attain a level of sophistication beyond trigonometry. In contrast, only 11 percent of high school students in California reach trigonometry. The college-bound Japanese generally take physics, chemistry, biology, and earth sciences, while in the U.S. many college-bound students assiduously and successfully avoid any such array of science courses.

This emphasis continues in college, with the result that Japan graduates more engineers from undergraduate college programs than does the U.S., despite the fact that their population is only half the size of ours. The U.S. produces Ph.D. researchers in numbers large enough to compete with Japan, but production of technicians in Japan outstrips that of the U.S. by a considerable margin. The Japanese are setting very high standards of scientific literacy for their entire school population and at the same time developing an intensive science and math track for their ablest students.

Japan also requires all of its high school students to take an extensive language and social studies curriculum, including ethics, civics, history, political science, and economics. All high school graduates must complete at least three years of social studies, whereas U.S. school districts generally require only two years. While Japan was increasing its social studies enrollments in the 1970s, the percentage of California high school students taking a social studies course in grades 7 through 12 declined from 71 percent to 45 percent—a drop of 575,000 students in one state alone.

The overall achievement scores of Japanese students in math and science are the highest in the non-Communist world. And Japanese pupils learn more social studies than do our students. How are they able to accomplish so much? One answer is *time*. The level of student achievement is directly related to the amount of time spent studying specific curricular content. If Group A spends twice as much time studying algebra as a similar group of students, Group B, then on the average Group A will show higher math achievement than Group B. Educational researchers use a specific phrase, *academic learning time*, to refer to the amounts of time that a student spends in learning tasks that yield high rates of success. Japanese schools spend much more time on academic tasks than do their U.S. counterparts. Their school year is longer by about one-third, and the Japanese high schools offer only a fraction of the non-academic electives that occupy—or clutter—the curriculum in the United States. If we compare the U.S. and Europe we find that the total time spent in elementary school is comparable. But when we get to the high school level, several European nations provide more instructional hours per year than we do (see Table 5-3).

Japanese students also spend far more time doing homework than do American students—nearly twice as many hours as their counterparts in California, for example. Japanese students know that their chances for economic success depend on being accepted at a good college. Few Japanese ever change employers after college, and the best jobs with the best companies go to graduates of the most competitive colleges. Universities in Japan select students according to high school grades and the results of rigorous college entrance examinations. Because competition for space in the better Japanese universities is so keen, some 45 percent of Japanese high school students attend after-school cramming sessions for college entrance exams. Thirty-nine percent of Japanese high school graduates go on to postsecondary education soon after high school, compared with 44 percent in the United States.

TABLE 5-3

A Comparison of Instructional Time in Nine Countries

	Instructional Hours per Day		Instructional Days per Year		Instructional Hours per Year	
	Primary	*Secondary*	*Primary*	*Secondary*	*Primary*	*Secondary*
Belgium	4.2	5.6	200	200	840	1,120
Finland	4.0	6.0	200	194	800	1,164
France	5.4	5.0	170	155	918	775
Germany (FDR)	3.3	4.0	230	230	759	920
Italy	5.0	5.8	175	195	875	1,131
Netherlands	5.2	5.6	200	200	1,040	1,120
Sweden	5.4	6.0	180	180	972	1,080
United Kingdom	5.0	5.0	180	180	900	900
United States	5.0	5.0	180	180	900	900

Source: A. Harry Passow et al., *The National Case Study: An Empirical Comparative Study of Twenty-one Educational Systems* (New York: Wiley and Sons, 1976).

Cultural Differences and School Performance

All these facts illustrate another truth: A comparison of student achievement and school performance is also a comparison of societies. In internationally based tests we have no way to adjust for such related variables as the homogeneity of the society and the social and economic condition of its members. For example, some researchers looking for the sources of the successful performance of Japan's school system have found a familiar figure—mother. Jerome Kagan, a psychologist at Harvard University, describes a typical family pattern:

> Until her child goes to school, the Japanese mother devotes herself to the rearing of the child. In verbal and nonverbal ways, she reminds the child of her deep, deep, warm feelings and that the child is the most important thing in the world to her. Then she says, "After all I've done for you, don't disappoint me." She's like the Jewish mother who says, "What do you mean you're not hungry—after I've slaved all day over a hot stove for you?"[3]

While we have chosen to emphasize the values of equality and individualism and thus the right of women to work outside the home, Japan tracks most of its women into the equivalent of the now passé American "finishing school," where the emphasis is on traditional homemaking skills.

Cultural differences also appear to affect differences in educational achievement within our own society. In 1975, the Educational Testing

Service, which develops the aptitude test used by many colleges to screen applicants, began to record test scores by ethnic group. The results showed that Asian-Americans, mainly Chinese, score about 45 points above the national average on the Scholastic Aptitude Test—higher than any other ethnic group. On the Graduate Record Exam, used to screen college graduates applying for advanced study, the same ethnic group averages about 55 points above the national norm in mathematics. Why? The *New York Times* of January 9, 1983, reports some answers. The dean of Cooper Union's School of Engineering, Dr. Chor-Wen Tan, cites love of education and a gift for detail and precision. He then says, "American children are trained to ask the question 'Why?' but Chinese children are taught to listen and to quietly reflect." A professor of mathematics and education at Pennsylvania State University emphasizes memorization—the traditional method of learning in China and a discipline useful in the study of mathematics. The chairman of Wang Laboratories in Massachusetts, Mr. An Wang, who was born and raised in Taiwan, suggests that the language itself may make mathematics seem more natural to Chinese: "In the Chinese language there is the one-syllable character, and Arabic numbers are also one syllable. Chinese may simply find it easier to read numbers than words." But the proclivity of students in the United States to ask "Why?" and to question traditional ways of doing things contributes to the innovative and entrepreneurial character of our nation. Each of these societal characteristics has benefits and costs.

Another international study also stresses cultural differences underlying differences in school performance. A study organized by the Center for Human Growth and Development at the University of Michigan and directed by Harold W. Stevenson compared achievement, behavior, and parental (maternal) attitudes for 5,000 young pupils—first-graders and fifth-graders—in 120 classrooms in each of three cities: Minneapolis, Minnesota; Taipei, Taiwan; and Sendai, Japan. At both grade levels, the American children scored poorly in mathematics. If children from the three cities had performed comparably, approximately 33 children from each country would have been among those receiving the top 100 scores. For American first-graders, the number was 15. (Sixteen percent of the first-graders could not count the 17 dots in one of the test questions.) For American fifth-graders, the number was one. In none of the 20 American fifth-grade classrooms studied did the children reach an average score on the

Japanese students taking a test. In mathematics and science Japanese students lead the non-Communist world in overall achievement scores.

mathematics test equivalent to that of the children in the worst-performing Japanese classroom. (Ten percent of the American fifth-graders could not divide 42 by 6, and 9 percent could not divide 24 by 3.) Although the American pupils scored better in reading than in math, the test scores for reading and vocabulary showed the American pupils over-represented among both the best and the worst readers.

Stevenson and his fellow observers also found that American children were far less attentive to the teacher and to their work than were the Japanese or Chinese children. They were more inclined to talk to their classmates, to ask irrelevant questions, to wander about the room, or simply to stare into space. At home, the Americans spent much less time on homework. They also watched more television and did more chores (see Figure 5-3). One Chinese mother, when asked why she did not assign her child any chores, responded, "It would break my heart to take him away from his studies." American mothers more frequently reported themselves satisfied with their children's progress in school than did the Chinese or Japanese mothers. American mothers were also more likely than their counterparts to credit school achievement to the child's natural ability. The Chinese—and especially the Japanese—mothers placed more emphasis upon the child's effort (see Figure 5-4).

Is Japan Our Best Model?

Even in Japan, however, educators acknowledge problems, and in some areas they look to our system for models. For example, Japan's math and science curriculum makes widespread use of instructional materials developed in the United States. It is ironic that the U.S. National Science Foundation developed the new physics, chemistry, and biology materials that the Japanese have adapted. These curricular materials are among the most challenging available, and Japan makes an enormous investment in keeping science teachers up-to-date. By contrast, the U.S. does very little in-service teacher training and is experiencing shortages of math and science teachers.

My direct observation of classroom teaching techniques in Japan reveals some weaknesses that the United States may be able to avoid. A persistent teaching strategy in Japan is the use of imitation and rote learning—methods considered outmoded by most educators in this country. In art classes, for example, students laboriously copy

FIGURE 5-3

Mothers' Estimates of How Children Spend Time Outside School

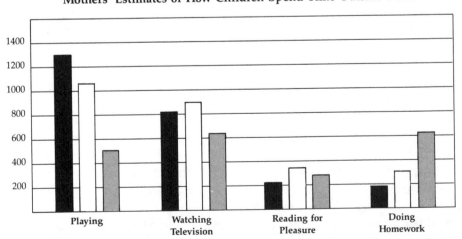

Source: Harold W. Stevenson, "Making the Grade: School Achievement in Japan, Taiwan, and the United States," *Journal of Educational Psychology* (June 1982).

■ United States   ☐ Japan   ▨ Taiwan

ancient ceramic treasures. Japanese high school students are judged on standardized tests primarily by their memorization of facts and concepts. Japanese teachers dispense knowledge, and the students dutifully write it down as unchallengeable truth. They do not use the school library creatively to weave together sources of information from which to formulate their own interpretations. This style of education is not noted for enhancing innovation or for fostering radical departures from accepted ways of thinking. On the other hand, Japanese children are taught that each repetition of a process contains something new. They learn to discriminate among tiny variations in routines, to "see the form, but see through the form to improve it." The Japanese record of improvement of imported technologies attests to the success of this philosophy.

Many in our country are more than a little envious of Japanese economic success and admire the schooling that enhances it. But we need not rush to copy the Japanese system. The educational achievements of that nation have been won at a high price. A major concern of the Japanese Ministry of Education is that academic competition is too intense. Officials are worried about the extent of psychological stress associated with the highly competitive college entrance ex-

FIGURE 5-4

Mothers' Ratings of Factors Contributing to Academic Success

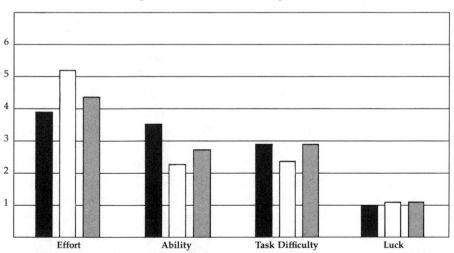

Source: Harold W. Stevenson, "Making the Grade: School Achievement in Japan, Taiwan, and the United States," *Journal of Educational Psychology* (June 1982).

■ United States ☐ Japan ▨ Taiwan

aminations. They fear that Japanese children are neglecting other aspects of their development, among them physical fitness. Getting into a good college is one of the few legitimate goals that Japanese society offers its young people (some say the only goal). Intense academic pressure also produces negative social effects. Not surprisingly, some nonachievers lose all sense of meaning in their lives and turn to truancy, gangs, and even suicide, partly because non-academic vocations command little prestige.

In assessing what these international tests tell us about how well schools perform in Japan or West Germany or any other country, we should remember the limitations of all tests. Tests are biased by the purposes for which they are designed. Some tests used in international comparisons were designed exclusively to select the most able students for entrance into a university. They were not designed to assess how well average students handle the material they have studied, nor were they meant to constitute an international School Achievement Olympics. In short, they do not perfectly match the schools' curricula, nor do they test how well the schools are performing the roles assigned to them in their respective societies.

Furthermore, tests can evaluate some areas of skill much better than others. To construct a test that would show how well the schools are doing in transmitting a common culture or how well students have learned their country's literature or history would call for remarkable feats of test engineering. Do French secondary schools do a better job of teaching Racine or Molière than the secondary schools in our country do of teaching Shakespeare? The answer would depend to some extent on the relative difficulty of the language of each writer. Which Japanese novelists compare best with Dickens or with Melville?

An analogy here from the world of sports illustrates the difficulty: Swimming and gymnastics are practiced in the same way throughout the world, but "football" means, variously, rugby, or soccer, or the activities of the NFL. Mathematics and science have the same characteristics wherever they are found, but literature varies in dozens of ways. Even "simple" assessments of reading are difficult to make. How can a test adjust for the varying degree of difficulty among national languages? If English comprises a greater total number of words than German or Japanese, is the task of learning to read it more difficult? How great a barrier to development of reading skills is the notorious phonetic irregularity of English spelling? Given the difficulty of creating an appropriate instrument to test students' skill in reading literature or history even in their native language, it is not surprising that international tests focus upon math and science. And because Japanese schools also focus on math and science, the tests are skewed toward the greatest strength of the Japanese curriculum. From this perspective, it is less surprising that Japanese test scores in these areas are outstanding. The international tests, then, show us a few things, but not what the newspapers sometimes report them as showing.

Declining Test Scores

But what about measurements made by our own tests, measurements that reveal a decline in students' scores over the past ten years? Reports on the declining scores of graduating high school seniors on the Scholastic Aptitude Test (SAT) have made news for a decade. As Table 5-4 indicates, there was a decline between 1966 and 1980, but this decline was arrested in 1981 and scores are now stable. The most recent tests (1984) even show some improvement. But the SAT tests were never meant to be a thermometer for the entire system of education in the United States. The SAT is designed to assess a pupil's potential or innate aptitude for college-level work, but it does not reflect what students have been taught in elementary and secondary schools. Also, because it tests only the college-bound population of the schools, it does not measure the performance of students at the low end of the band of academic achievement. An immense number of such students could have improved their skills over the same period of time, but the SAT would record nothing of this achievement.

A more comprehensive study of performance is the National Assessment of Educational Progress (NAEP). Initiated in 1969, the NAEP is funded by the U.S. government and administered by the Educational Testing Service in Princeton, New Jersey. The NAEP includes all students, not just those who are college bound, and it measures what students have actually learned. The NAEP shows that between 1973 and 1980, the average score in mathematics earned by 17-year-olds declined 3.6 percentage points (see Table 4-9). On the other hand, from 1974 to 1980, the reading scores of 9-year-olds increased by 2.6 percentage points (see Table 4-8). The NAEP, then, agrees with the SAT in recording a decline in mathematical skill among seniors in secondary school, but it also records the schools' success with younger pupils.

TABLE 5-4

Scholastic Aptitude Test Score Averages
for College-Bound High School Seniors, 1966–81

	1966-67	1970-71	1975-76	1978-79	1980-81
Average Verbal Scores					
Male	463	454	433	431	430
Female	468	457	430	423	418
Total	466	455	431	427	424
Average Mathematical Scores					
Male	514	507	497	493	492
Female	467	466	446	443	443
Total	492	488	472	467	466

Sources: Department of Education, National Center for Education Statistics, *Digest of Education Statistics* (Washington, D.C.: U.S. Government Printing Office, 1980, 1982); College Entrance Examination Board, *National Report, College Bound Seniors* (New York: CEEB, 1981).

The SAT, designed to assess a pupil's potential for college-level work, does not directly reflect what students have been taught in elementary and secondary school. Declining scores (now stabilized) have been news for a decade, even though the test does not accurately reflect the performance of the schools.

NAEP results do, however, emphasize the growing weakness in U.S. students' attainment of "higher order skills." U.S. youngsters can comprehend short paragraphs but have great difficulty with longer, complex passages, particularly with respect to interpreting the tone and mood of the author. U.S. children do well in repetitive math problems like multiplication tables but are losing ground in math problem solving. This includes the application of mathematical formulas or concepts to problems or contexts that the student has not been drilled on or seen before. (Table 4-9 demonstrates the large gains made by black pupils compared to white since 1970, but there is still a considerable gap to close.)

In short, the age group more fully under the influence of the school, the 9-year-olds, improved in a key academic skill, while that group most likely to be influenced by peers, to abuse drugs and alcohol, and to cut class—the teenagers—has lost ground in mathematics. This way of interpreting the facts is obviously biased, but it is meant to be—to illustrate how little these tests take into account social and cultural conditions.

Between 1968 and 1974 the NAEP reported a considerable drop in U.S. science achievement scores—and it has not been reversed in later tests. Ralph Tyler, former director of the Center for Advanced Study in the Behavioral Sciences at Stanford, argued that there is a correspondence between public attitudes toward science and the average level of science achievement among 17-year-olds. According to this view, negative public attitudes about science turned many students away from science. At the time of the first national assessment in 1969, the U.S. public was enthusiastic about our space program and its technological achievements. But by 1974, when scores dropped, reports of air and water pollution, of excessive exploitation of natural resources, and of the harmful effects of technology had brought about a decline in the prestige of science.

The NAEP does, however, document a significant achievement for American education—one I have already called attention to in Chapter 4: The scores for black students registered gains in achievement, especially for students with low scores in math. This group showed a substantial improvement between 1972 and 1980 in elementary and middle schools (see Table 4-9). Thus, although 13-year-olds in general made lower scores on the mathematical assessment in 1980 than in 1973, black students raised their scores over the same period, with low achievers showing greater gains than high achievers.

This gain was not spontaneous or accidental. During the 1970s, the federal and state governments placed a high priority on improving the achievement of disadvantaged students, particularly Blacks in the Southeast. Title I of the federal Elementary and Secondary School Act provided compensatory education programs such as remedial reading and math. Many of these programs employed specialist teachers who worked intensively with small groups of pupils. The nation persisted in this objective from 1965 to 1980, and by 1972, when the Title I program was seven years old, the major positive results were already manifest. By the 1980s, the achievement tests measured a significant gain for the group aided through Title I. The lesson is clear: When we define our goals and pursue them—with patience—we can improve our schools' performance.

Evaluating the Tests

Both the international tests and the NAEP tests assess only the most academic, the most intellectual, areas of learning. International testing leaves many questions unanswered. Do American pupils have higher self-esteem, better citizenship skills, or more creativity? Do our students know more about potential career choices and enjoy more enriching leisure activities? How do our young musicians and artists fare in international competitions? The international tests cannot tell us. Have courses in driver's education lowered the number of arrests for reckless driving or reduced the number of accidents? Does school improve our students' health and eating habits? When our pupils become adults do they spend more of their leisure time in reading? The international tests cannot tell us. Nor can the national tests. All of these questions focus on goals that are important for sections of the American public, but we do not assess whether the schools are meeting them. To boil down the performance rating of our schools to the SAT measure of college aptitude for one-third of the graduating high school students is ridiculous. A headline in the *Los Angeles Times* of April 15, 1984, sums up the situation: "U.S. Schools Lack a Yardstick to Measure Performance—A Sticky Situation."

Nor does it make sense to believe that international tests have revealed so great a weakness in our schools that it threatens our economic standing in the world. The catalyst of an earlier crisis—the orbiting of Sputnik—revealed, among other things, that President Eisenhower and Defense Secretary Wilson had chosen not to accelerate our manned space program in order to concentrate on other uses of rockets. But the schools ended up among the main villains when the Soviet Sputnik launch beat the U.S. timetable. Similarly, Japan's emergence as an economic threat to the U.S. can be traced to the history of the American steel and auto industries as well as to the American school system. To expect the school system to solve problems of rigidity and low quality in our industrial economy is once again to expect public education to solve every social problem from alcoholism to unemployment.

The objective of international testing is not to create a quasi-Olympics but to work toward the design of instruments to measure school performance. If we pull back from a competitive and crisis-ridden view of the results of these tests, we can learn much that is useful. For example, we can learn that when adjustments are made for our larger enrollments, schools in Europe do not appear to prepare students better than we do. We learn, too, that our best students compare favorably with the best in any country. And, perhaps most important of all, we learn that the only other nation to have over 75 percent of its pupils enrolled in high school has a record of high academic achievement. That an egalitarian system like Japan's reaches a high level of academic achievement ought to be good news, given the importance of equality in our system of values.

It is not good news, however, to learn that the gap in academic educational achievement between Japan and our nation is increasing. But we know that the goals of Japanese schooling do not include vocational or personal development. Japanese schools limit themselves to academic objectives, and they commit more time to those objectives. Their school year is 240 days, as compared to the U.S. school year of 175 days. West German schools also limit their objectives and seem to accomplish these goals even though their school day is shorter than ours. From these comparisons and from the success of our Title I programs of the 1970s, we can draw encouraging conclusions that support one of the major themes of this book: If we reduce the number of objectives that our schools pursue, and if we show patience and persistence as the schools pursue those goals, we can improve the performance of the public schools and raise the level of our students' academic achievement.

CHAPTER

DOLLARS
AND
DECISIONS

Neither the word "education" nor the word "school" appears in the Constitution of the United States. Because the framers chose not to include education among the functions of the federal government, the provision of schooling is a power reserved to the states. State constitutions acknowledge this responsibility, and a succession of court decisions has reinforced the states' plenary authority in education. The courts support the right of state government to abolish any school district, or to take over its management and to dismiss local officials.

Despite the legal primacy of state government, important decision-making power has been delegated by states to local school district officials. Traditionally, Americans have feared distant government; they have wanted important decisions made close to home. In the nineteenth century, local control was also a practical necessity. Before modern communications technology became available, it was not possible to administer schools dispersed across the state from a central office in the capital. Few components of American political ideology are as firmly ingrained as local control of the schools—a "minor branch of theology," former California State Superintendent of Education Wilson Riles called it. In every state but Hawaii, which has a history of centralized royal authority, the legislature has delegated powers to the local school boards. At one time, decision-making power rested in some 130,000 local school districts. At present they number about 16,000.

The system of local control has many advantages—foremost among them, flexibility and adaptability. The ability of local authorities to

"Scylla or Charibdis?" The cover from a 1915 issue of *The School Board Journal*.

adapt the tone and style of schools to the desires of local clients largely accounts for the widespread acceptance of public schooling in the United States. American public schools serve 90 percent of the eligible school-age population, and private schools the remaining 10 percent. It is not likely that a centralized school system, with its almost inescapable pressures toward uniformity and standardization, would have succeeded in meeting the desires of such widely divergent constituent elements. Another advantage of decentralization lies in the ability of individual units to experiment without jeopardizing the stability of an entire system. "Lighthouse" schools and districts, by virtue of their willingness to test new ideas, often set the standard for surrounding districts and, according to some, elevate the quality of education throughout the nation.

The American pattern of decentralization has also made for some serious disadvantages. In the absence of uniform standards and a strong central authority some districts may offer inferior schooling. In some instances, local residents may themselves be too uneducated to judge the quality of instruction in their schools. In other instances, a local elite may exercise its power by refusing to provide the schools with adequate financing. Recently, school boards in Chicago, Cleveland, and San Jose, California, permitted their districts to go bankrupt. Presumably, a more centralized school governance arrangement could enforce higher standards throughout each state and ensure each district's fiscal integrity.

As a principle, local control remains unchallenged. In fact, however, a change in governance has been taking place. Some observers even contend that the growing influence of centralizing forces—state and federal authorities, courts, national testing agencies, and nationwide interest groups—has made "home rule" now more illusion than actuality.

Who Pays for Public Education?

Americans adhere to the view that "decisions follow the dollar." If this view is correct, then the change by which states have increased their financing of education is a radical one. In 1930, the local property tax provided 83 cents of every dollar used to finance the schools. By 1980 this amount had declined to 43 cents. As Table 6-1 illustrates, the major share of financial responsibility has fallen upon the state governments. Elementary and secondary education now absorb 58 percent of all state aid to local governments. This growth in financial

TABLE 6-1

Sources of Public School Revenue Receipts, 1929-80

	1929-30	1939-40	1949-50	1959-60	1969-70	1979-80
Total Revenue Receipts (in billions of dollars)	$2.09	$2.26	$5.44	$14.75	$40.27	$96.90
Percent of Revenue from:						
Federal Government	0.4	1.8	2.9	4.4	8.0	9.8
State Governments	16.9	30.2	39.8	39.1	39.9	46.8
Local Sources	82.7	68.0	57.3	56.5	52.1	43.4

Source: Department of Education, National Center for Education Statistics, *Digest of Education Statistics* (Washington, D.C.: U.S. Government Printing Office, 1980, 1981, 1982).

State governments have assumed an ever-increasing share of public financing.

responsibility has been paralleled by a growth in the states' control of school policy.

While the 1960s were a decade of federal innovation in education, the 1970s and 1980s belong to the states. In the 1970s many state legislatures added staff, thus enlarging their capacity for policy research. Many now meet annually or for more extended sessions than in earlier years. Legislators thus have the resources to formulate and oversee education policy. Many governors now have their own specialists in education and finance. Also, many states have expanded their fiscal capacity. Between 1960 and 1979, eleven states adopted a personal income tax, nine a corporate income tax, and ten a general sales tax. Thirty-seven states drew on all three of these revenue sources in 1979, compared to just 19 in 1960. State income taxes provided 35 percent of all tax revenue in 1978, compared to 19 percent in 1969. This diversification of their revenue systems has increased the states' capacity to provide educational and other services.

The power of state education agencies to intercede in local school policy has also increased dramatically. Ironically, the federal government provided the initial impetus for this expansion. The Elementary and Secondary Education Act of 1965 (ESEA) and its subsequent amendments required state agencies to approve local projects requesting federal funds for educational innovation and education for disadvantaged, handicapped, bilingual, and migrant children. In such federally funded programs, 1 percent of the money was earmarked for state administration. Title V of ESEA also provided general support for state administrative resources, giving some priority to state planning and evaluation. The expansion in California's state agency between 1964 and 1970 was financed wholly by federal funds. In 1972, 70 percent of the funding for the state education agency in Texas came from federal aid. New staff capacity was available to state administrators or state boards that chose to take an active role in local education. By 1972, three-fourths of the staff members in state agencies of education had been in their jobs for less than three years.

Confusion among traditional supporters of local control has also strengthened the move toward centralization. Teachers' unions, school boards, and administrators' associations can no longer agree on common policies with parent organizations and others of their old allies. As they feud among themselves, they create a vacuum of power that activists within state governments can exploit. Loss of public confidence in professional educators and the decline in achievement scores have also provoked many legislators to contend that local school employees should have much less discretion.

The 1970s also saw large-scale expansion in the influence of state courts over education policy. In 1968, state education authorities in California were sued only four times; in the first ten months of 1980, they were sued 34 times. In 1981, as president of the California State Board of Education, I was a defendant in 108 active lawsuits. In most of these suits, plaintiffs wanted the State Board to intervene in local affairs—for example, to force reluctant local school boards to offer more bilingual education, or to provide expensive hospital services for handicapped children. In resolving conflicts like these, the courts have served as a stimulus to more state control. Even more significantly, they have brought within their scope questions of school financing, for they have stimulated and furthered a process designed to overcome the inequities created by the local property tax.

Inequities in School Financing: The Property Tax

Vast differences in local property wealth have meant vast differences in funds available to schools and in the property tax rates that generate those funds. A comparison of two school districts in Oregon shows how inequities can arise from the financing of public education through taxes on property. In 1975, the Brothers school district had an assessed value of property of $537,761 per pupil. In contrast, Knox Butte school district was restricted to a tax base of $16,119 in assessed value of property for every pupil. Obviously, the Brothers school district could provide a plush educational program even with a very low property

A rural American classroom, Kentucky, 1940.

tax rate, while Knox Butte would have to tax itself at a very high property tax rate to mount even the minimum state program. To fund schools by a property tax means that property-rich districts receive a double benefit: They have more money to spend on their schools than property-poor districts and they enjoy a lower tax rate besides. "Equity" among taxpayers would mean that an equal tax effort produces an equal sum of money per pupil. The property tax fails to achieve this equity.

In the 1970s, many believed that the American dream of equal opportunity necessitated high quality school services for all children—that schooling is crucial to personal success and societal harmony. This general belief became an articulated social concern through the efforts of social scientists and legal scholars who, in writing and in court, questioned the constitutionality of many state school finance arrangements. These reformers contended that the taxation and distribution schemes of most states violated the equal protection clause of the Fourteenth Amendment of the United States Constitution. The Supreme Court, by a five to four vote, disagreed with this position (*San Antonio v. Rodriguez*, 1973). Nevertheless, a number of state lower courts found the argument compelling on state constitutional grounds. Thus, the legal and political movement toward financial equality was sustained, though at the state rather than the national level. In 1973 alone, 11 states, either as the result of court decisions, or in the face of pending suits, significantly altered their methods of generating and distributing funds for schools. Oregon, as we have seen, did not.

Continued challenges to the property tax, reinforced by growing reluctance among voters to support higher tax rates for school measures, led President Nixon during his first term seriously to consider a policy proposal that would have replaced school property tax revenues with proceeds from a federal sales tax. Although by the mid-1970s the pendulum of opinion had begun to swing back in favor of the property tax, the short-lived period of criticism had done much to focus the attention of policymakers on the inequities of property tax administration. Using sophisticated computer technology to simulate the revenue and distributional consequences of a proposed plan, several states, among them Florida and Utah, have made significant strides toward implementing a finance plan that achieves greater equity in expenditures per pupil. Other states, for example, West Virginia and New Jersey, are under court order to establish more equitable finance arrangements.

Designing a school finance scheme that meets a strict test of fiscal equity is fairly easy. But designing a plan that both meets that test and simultaneously satisfies the various interest groups concerned with school financing and its effects—that is a rigorous undertaking. An obvious solution to the problem of inequity between the two Oregon school districts would be for the state to eradicate the inequity by providing much more state aid for Knox Butte than for Brothers. In 1975, however, Oregon gave each of these school districts identical amounts of financial assistance per pupil, because grants of the same size were easier to sustain in the Oregon political system.

In many states, such disparities have been tolerated for fear that their correction would bring about state dominance of education. The argument runs like this: "Decisions always follow the dollar. If the state plays a larger role in financing schools, then the state will play a larger role in deciding matters such as curriculum content, personnel policies, and discipline practices. State dominance and the consequent erosion of local control would risk uniform indoctrination and ideological standardization. The only means of restricting unwarranted state intrusion in local matters and preserving independence is to continue to fund schools principally from local resources." Where this argument has prevailed, the result has been a weak state role in school finance and the persistence of inequitable financing conditions.

Inequities in School Financing: Regional Differences

The property tax is the chief cause of inequities in school financing, but in many localities economic hardship derives from special circumstances. Florida presents a typical case, together with a state-level solution to the problem. Like several other states, Florida contains two or more economic regions within its boundaries, and the cost of living varies from region to region. Under such circumstances, equal school expenditures may not buy equal school services. Florida annually conducts a cost-of-living survey for each of the state's 67 counties. In 1972, when Florida dramatically revised its school finance arrangements, the state cost-of-living index (with a mean of 1.0) ranged from a low of .87 near the Georgia border to a high of 1.2 near Miami. A cost index multiplier was incorporated into Florida's finance plan to adjust for regional differences in purchasing power, and districts with extraordinarily higher costs of living were granted added fiscal resources.

The distribution of population in a state can also create economic hardship. A sparse population can be costly. Not only must children be bused farther in sparsely settled areas, but school districts must maintain smaller schools, and these are not economical. As a consequence, many state formulas provide added financial resources for small, isolated school districts. Such provisions are in keeping with a goal of providing the same amount of school resources for each child in a state.

The composition of the student population also varies. Some districts serve a disproportionate number of mentally or physically handicapped children. Obviously, providing these children with anything close to equal educational opportunity necessitates a substantial increase in expenditure. Policymakers now recognize, too, that severe economic deprivation can impair a child's ability to learn. Compensatory education programs have been designed to assist such children in learning, but because these programs often call for instruction to be given individually or in small groups, they are costly.

City School Districts

If children who need extra educational services are not evenly distributed across all school districts, neither are they distributed at random. By 1978 every one of the nine largest city school systems had an enrollment of more than 60 percent minority students. Urban populations include the poor and disadvantaged in disproportionate numbers; children in such groups—often as a consequence of poor diet and inadequate prenatal and medical care—suffer from learning disabilities that require expensive programs of compensatory education. City school districts, then, are often forced to spend more than suburban ones.

Before the 1970s, patterns of state politics intensified this situation by preventing cities from seeking fiscal relief. Electoral district boundaries did not reflect the nation's population shift from rural to urban areas, and rural agricultural interests continued to dominate many state legislatures. Court decisions mandating the redistricting of

congressional and state political jurisdictions have had a profound influence upon the geographic distribution of political power. The suburbs have benefited most from redistricting, but cities, too, have acquired a significant bloc of legislative votes. Although New York City, Chicago, Los Angeles, and Denver do not control an absolute majority of votes in their respective state legislatures, they now have sufficiently large blocs of votes to defeat many legislative proposals. Thus political reality now makes it necessary to accommodate urban interests in the area of school finance reform.

City spokespeople believe they have a good case for extra attention in school finance matters. Not only do cities contain more children who require special educational services than smaller localities, but they are obliged to deal with what is frequently and aptly labeled "municipal overburden." Cities generally are forced to support more costly public services than surrounding areas—larger police departments, for example, and more welfare, parks, and centers for performing arts. Moreover, many of the services are used by nonresidents who contribute no tax revenue. The overall city tax rate—including school taxes—is often higher than that of suburbs and rural areas. Because of the wide range of noneducational services cities must subsidize, the high urban tax rate does not benefit schools, even though the property tax base of cities is usually higher than the state average.

A city that neatly fits this urban pattern is Detroit, Michigan, the largest and politically most influential city in its state. In addition to the usual urban problems, Detroit has a declining school-age population, a circumstance that directly reduces state revenues. Detroit is caught in a vise between rising school costs and a population unwilling or unable to meet those costs. The overwhelming majority of Detroit's voters no longer have children of school age, and they appear increasingly reluctant to tax themselves for school support.

Detroit's legislative representatives believe that the state should assist the city in meeting school expenses, because schooling is a state responsibility. They argue that Detroit's income tax and business tax contributions are a great asset to the state, and that it would be only fair for a larger share of the city's contributions to be returned to their source.

Detroit and many cities like it need an adequate and equitable system of school financing. Yet if the state funds public schools, what

TABLE 6-2

**Current Expenditures per Pupil in Public
Elementary and Secondary Schools, 1929-30 to 1979-80**

School Year	Unadjusted Dollars	Adjusted Dollars*
1929-30	$ 87	$ 373
1939-40	88	458
1949-50	209	633
1959-60	375	926
1969-70	816	1,569
1977-78	2,002	2,315
1979-80	2,275	2,396

*1979 purchasing power based on the consumer price index.

Source: Department of Education, National Center for Statistics, *Digest of Education Statistics* (Washington, D.C.: U.S. Government Printing Office, 1980, 1982).

becomes of local control? Understandably, many state legislators prefer to evade the issue.

Rising Costs in Public Education

Issues of equity are not the only thorny issues in school finance reform. School costs have soared in the last several decades. More precisely, while they have been declining as a share of GNP, costs have risen sharply in terms of dollars. Health and defense costs have risen even faster than the cost of education, but measured in dollar amounts, or as a portion of state and local government budgets, schooling has become an increasingly costly governmental service (see Tables 6-2 and 6-3).

Given the fact of rising costs, school finance reform almost inevitably necessitates higher levels of school spending. In order to achieve even minimal fiscal equity among districts and financial viability within them, legislators must enable low-spending districts to spend more—a process usually termed "leveling up." Of course, fiscal equity might be achieved by reducing expenditures in high-spending districts, but political reality in most states renders such reductions highly improbable. Leveling up means more dollars for schools. In California, I supported a state finance formula now in force that increases the revenue of low-spending districts like East Palo Alto by 10 percent a year, while the revenue of high-spending districts like Palo Alto increases at 4 percent a year.

TABLE 6-3

Gross National Product (GNP) Related to Current Expenditures for Public Elementary and Secondary Education, 1949–81

Year	GNP	Expenditures for Education		Expenditures for Health		Expenditures for Defense	
		Total	%/GNP	Total	%/GNP	Total	%/GNP
		(in billions/unadjusted dollars)					
1949	258.0	$ 4.7	1.8%	$ 11.6	4.5%	$ 13.2	5.1%
1959	486.5	12.3	2.5	24.9	5.1	45.6	9.4
1969	935.5	34.2	3.7	64.8	6.9	76.3	8.2
1975	1,528.8	62.1	4.1	131.5	8.6	83.7	5.5
1979	2,395.4	95.4	4.0	192.4[a]	9.1[a]	99.5[a]	4.7[a]
1981	2,925.5[b]	97.5[c]	3.3	247.2[b]	9.4	188.8[c]	6.5

[a] Figures are for 1978, based on the 1978 GNP of $2,106.6.
[b] Figures are for 1980, based on the 1980 GNP of $2,626.1.
[c] Based on estimates.

Source: Department of Commerce, Bureau of the Census, *Statistical Abstract of the United States* (Washington D.C.: U.S. Government Printing Office, 1980).

As a percentage of GNP, expenditures for education have dropped, while expenditures for health and defense have risen.

School finance statutes in most states are hopelessly complicated. Typically, only a few staff members in the legislative and executive branches really understand a state's arrangements. Legislators, educators, and the public are generally mystified by the legal technicalities surrounding the interaction of state and local school finance procedures. This complexity presents a special problem to reformers. To build enough support to pass the legislature, a plan must be sufficiently simple to be understood. On the other hand, accommodating the conflicting interests and values we have been describing entails some statutory complexity. State school finance formulas are like the United States tax code—voluminous, complex, and interwoven with numerous political bargains.

The Financial Carrot

Most policymakers recognize the necessity for added school dollars, but not surprisingly, at all levels of government they have been demanding evidence of greater school productivity. A large number of state statutes and local district plans have been devised in response to this movement, known fashionably as "accountability," a militant insistence that the schools take full responsibility for students' achievement or lack of it. To be successful, advocates of finance reform must devise means for assuring efficient use of school dollars.

A conventional approach to this problem has been to impose upon schools a model of technical efficiency adopted from industry. For example, merit pay would compensate teachers for high test scores among their students. Schools are viewed as an assembly line where teachers respond to fiscal incentives or sanctions and, in an orderly, predictable manner, accordingly produce children chock-full of facts. But first-rate teaching is a matter of personal talent, much closer to an art than to a repetitive assembly line. Teachers are more like coaches than like shop foremen; they need to stimulate students to ask questions and thereby cultivate the capacity for critical thought. Tests do not easily measure this kind of good teaching, and certainly most national tests do not measure a student's ability to tear apart a fallacious argument.

Imposing an industrial model on the schools is not the only way a state can express its legitimate interest in education. For example, a state legislature concerned that school districts maintain at least minimal performance standards for pupils may link economic incentives to its formula for distributing revenue. Both California and Florida will pay considerably more money per pupil in 1985 to those localities whose high school students improve their test scores well above the statewide average. In the past, some states offered school districts financial incentives to establish secondary schools; now, some induce districts to establish pre-schools for ages three to five. Added state resources can be a "carrot" leading local districts to revise or add programs.

Balancing State Financing and Local Control

Some who defend local control, including local financing, do not acknowledge the possibility that funding and decision making can be separated. In principle, the generation and distribution of school dollars can be centralized, while the decision-making authority remains decentralized. State equalization payments could be made to local schools with no strings attached. Yet the balance between the state's constitutionally specified authority to provide education and the public's view that school decisions should be made by local units of government is always a delicate one. Regardless of potential benefits for schoolchildren and taxpayers, any school finance plan that jeopardizes the balance of decision-making power is politically doomed.

To accommodate the strong political support for home rule while offering ways to overcome inequities in the present system, I recommend methods of school financing that emphasize local control over financial decisions. In particular, the concept of local guaranteed yield allows for the retention of local control over expenditure levels and tax rates, while establishing financial equity between districts. Under this system, the state government provides an ample, fully state-funded minimum education program for every district. By vote of the local school board or electorate, however, districts can levy a property tax to add to this state floor. At the same time, by a formula for redistributing funds, the state assures that every local school district choosing to spend more money expends the same tax effort for each dollar it adds to the state floor. The state assures that each additional dollar in property tax, locally approved, raises the same amount per pupil in every district in the state, whether the area has a great deal of property wealth or almost none.

A hypothetical case will illustrate how such a system works: Suppose that each of two California school districts, East Palo Alto and Palo Alto, votes to increase its property tax rate by $1 per $100 of assessed valuation. Suppose, further, that property wealth in the two districts differs, so that the tax increase yields only $100 per pupil in East Palo Alto but $300 per pupil in Palo Alto. Suppose, too, that the state already assures each school district a floor of $200 per pupil to spend. If nothing further is done, the tax levies in Palo Alto and East Palo Alto—levies representing the same tax effort of $1 per $100 of assessed valuation—will result in East Palo Alto's having $300 to spend per pupil while Palo Alto has $500 to spend. At this point, under the concept of local guaranteed yield, the state will redistribute to East Palo Alto some of the funds raised in Palo Alto, so that both districts have the same additional amount above the state minimum to spend—in our hypothetical case, $200 above the state floor, or $400 per pupil. In this way, the same tax effort raises each district to the same level above the guaranteed state minimum.

Despite the difficulties it poses, school finance reform must continue. Under the current system, too many taxpayers are subject to property tax rates that reflect only the value of property in their district—not their desire to tax themselves for education or their ability to pay. And too many students throughout the United States continue to be victimized merely because their parents reside in a school jurisdiction with low property wealth. Schooling is too important to be left to chance distributions of wealth and to public policies that capriciously ignore economic realities. School financing is, however, enmeshed in the web of complicated and conflicting economic values, social philosophies, and political interests analyzed throughout this book. Any proposal for reform, in order to succeed, must balance these competing forces.

C H A P T E R

WHO SHAPES THE CURRICULUM?

A focus on school financing reveals a tug of war between state and local forces, between central and local control. But to attempt a reasonably complete answer to the question, Who controls the schools? we must extend our analysis. As we do so, we find that education policy is more like a net pulled by a crowd in many directions at once than like a thick rope tugged at by opposing forces. The school curriculum—what should be taught, from what textbooks and by what methods—is constantly being reshaped.

Professional educators often speak as if the curriculum were a thing apart from—and to be shielded from—politics. That they regard the curriculum as a "professional" matter, however, does not insulate their opinions from the major social concerns that have always influenced the curriculum in American schools—the need or desire for religious training, Americanization, occupational training, and so on. But the needs of society are not their sole concern. As professionals, they differ among themselves in the criteria they apply to curricular decisions; among these are tradition, the results of scientific testing, common social values, and individual judgment. Lack of agreement on the required content and intellectual level of school curricula is also the rule among the diverse state and local authorities. In view of the differences in the composition of their populations and in their values, this is hardly surprising.

Shapers of the Curriculum

Although no universally accepted criteria for curricular decisions exist, there has been rough agreement to teach certain subjects: English, history, science, mathematics, and health. Social studies and foreign languages, though less firmly established, also meet with wide approval. The loose consensus on this matter is usually supported by several interested groups:

- School accrediting and testing agencies (private groups that function in the public sphere)
- Schools of education (often inertia-bound to the traditional curriculum)
- State boards of education and state departments of education (which must by law oversee a host of past and current policy decisions)

These groups tend to support an established or traditional curriculum. Others seek curricular changes. Publishers, although they maintain a heavy investment in existing textbooks, are swayed by interest and pressure groups to develop new instructional materials, which they try to sell to local or state authorities. The federal government has been a source of curriculum change; in the early 1970s, for example, half the schools were using a physics course newly developed with federal research funding, and about two-thirds were using a new biology course. Private foundations such as Ford and Carnegie also stimulate research that eventuates in new curricula and teaching materials. Professional associations of scientists and other scholarly, business, and professional groups engage in such research as well. And, always, university professors generate ideas about curriculum change. None of these groups, of course, speaks with a single voice.

At the local level, school boards, teachers, administrators, and parents may feel strongly about changing some element of the curriculum to fit prevailing local values, and despite central control of curriculum in some states (particularly the Southeast) these local authorities can prevail. Local opposition frequently takes intensely emotional form. Evolution, the United Nations, the role of racial minorities, and the social nature of humankind are subjects that have aroused passionate controversy. In each case, local people have sought to block either state directives or professionally accepted norms of "good" curriculum.

During the 1970s and early 1980s, local control of curriculum became an explosive issue in many areas. From 1970 to 1975, efforts to ban

"Education: The Nation's Safeguard for the Future."

books doubled over the preceding five years. In 1981 the American Library Association reported three to five episodes a week. Among these were the banning of Ken Kesey's *One Flew Over the Cuckoo's Nest* in Idaho Falls and Richard Wright's *Black Boy* in Anaheim, California. After the Warsaw, Indiana, school board banned 40 copies of *Values Clarification*, a popular text in social studies, the school board president posed the essential political question: Who shall control the minds of the students?

TABLE 7-1

Influences on Curriculum Policy Making

	National	*State*	*Local*
General Legislative	Congress	State Legislature	City Council (usually has no influence)
Educational Legislative	U.S. House Committee on Education & Labor	State School Board	Local School Board
Executive	President	Governor	Mayor (usually has no influence)
Administrative School	U.S. Department of Education	State Department of Education	Superintendent
Bureaucratic	National Science Foundation (Division of Curriculum Improvement)	State Department of Education (Division of Instruction)	Department Chairmen, Teachers
Professional Association	National Testing Agencies such as Educational Testing Service (ETS)	Accrediting Associations; State Subject Matter Affiliates, National Education Association	County Association of Superintendents
Private Interests	Foundations & Business Corporations, Political & Service Organizations		

Source: Frederick Wirt and Michael Kirst, *Political and Social Foundations of Education* (Berkeley, California: McCutchan Publishing Corporation, 1972).

The advocacy of new ideas about instructional methods and materials also forms part of a more general challenge—the challenge to the once unquestioned dominance of school policy by professionals. Although the larger picture shows that local authorities tend to accept the decisions of professionals, powerful political local forces, such as advocates of the creation story, can always intrude on and sometimes override professional policy. Table 7-1 summarizes the complex political web in which the making of curricular policy is caught. It lists a representative group of actors in the process of school governance.

Two case studies illustrate the full complexity of the process by which curricular policy is established: (1) how one state, California, recently chose new textbooks in history, and (2) how in an earlier decade the "new math" entered—and left—the school curriculum across the nation.

Case Study in Policy Making: Who Chooses Textbooks?

Textbooks are a major support of the school curriculum; two national surveys have confirmed that teachers use textbooks more than 70 percent of their instructional time. If all commercially developed instructional materials—including, for example, such items as film strips—are counted as "textbooks," the figure rises to between 90 and 95 percent. In response to the many influences on public school curriculum, publishers "manage" the process of textbook creation in this way: After studying the market and the texts currently in use, the publisher selects a writing team to prepare a series of texts. The team includes the publisher's internal editor, who is frequently the actual author of the book, although other authors are listed on the title page. Teachers' expressed instructional preferences and practices enter into the content of textooks, but teachers themselves rarely write texts. In fact, materials devised by teachers account for a startlingly low percentage of the instructional materials employed in the classroom.

The process of textbook adoption was new to me when I joined the California State Board of Education. Initially, I favored "open adoption"—that is, letting school districts themselves choose textbooks for the 4.25 million diverse pupils in California. By the end of two terms on the board, I was leading the way toward a policy more restrictive than the one then in force.

California is one of 15 states that adopt texts on a statewide basis; exclusion from the subject list in any of these states rules out most sales opportunities for a publisher's books on the particular subject in that entire state. Consequently, these states exercise a disproportionate influence on the national market. More than two-thirds of the states that follow this procedure lie within the former Confederacy or border upon it. Texas, owing to its size and to its unique payment-in-advance financing formula, has more influence on what is published than any other state.

In California, the ten-member state board, selected for four-year terms by the governor, serves as the final authority. The board delegates the technical analysis of texts to a 16-person advisory curriculum commission. Subject matter specialists selected for the commission— usually two for each field (science, reading, and so on)—play a major role in defining the content of their disciplines. More often than not, they decide what students should learn in the limited time available and determine the best techniques for conveying that body of knowledge. They also have the responsibility for appointing three regional panels, each composed of 20 educators for every subject area, to assist in evaluating instructional materials. The curriculum commission recommends specific books to the state board, which members of the board review before each monthly meeting.

California rotates adoptions, every six years approving new texts for a particular subject field like history. Each cycle—from appointing a commission, to establishing "frameworks" (criteria for selection), to reviewing and adopting texts—takes as long as two years to complete. In the late 1970s, the system was one of "multiple adoptions"; that is, the board approved a lengthy and extensive list of books from which local districts then made their selections. Once books are placed on the state list, publishers still must convince local districts to buy them with money allotted by the state. In 1983 California provided $80.5 million for textbook purchases.

A Complex Process

The first step in this process, appointing the commission of specialists, proved difficult. Few members of the state board knew experts or outstanding teachers in every subject field. Often they had to rely on recommendations from someone they had only "heard about." In any case, members of the board had little information about how a potential commissioner might evaluate texts for content and pedagogy. (They did, however, know how candidates stood on "creation science," the issue that dominated board meetings from 1975 to 1978.) Each subject area has its major issues and teaching concerns about which, not surprisingly, lay board members know little. Yet, to judge texts critically, board members needed to understand technical concepts particular to each field, concepts like "questioning strategies," "multisensory approaches," and "Cloze reading techniques."

Curriculum commission members were guided by (1) a curricular framework consisting of general statements about a subject, and (2) specific criteria laid down for textbook publishers, such as print size and the quality of paper to be used. In 1975, frameworks for the subject field of reading included such broad statements of goal as these: "An imagination that is broadened beyond the confines of the pupil's world through exploring literature." Such criteria were far too vague to allow for screening out texts on the basis of content or coverage. In effect, the various members of the curriculum commission decided whether the content of a textbook in their specialty was appropriate. At the beginning of my tenure, so little attention was devoted to content that the guidelines did not even require that the texts be carefully checked to assure that their content was aligned with questions on the statewide achievement tests. Nor was information gathered to let the board know how students reacted to different texts. The focus was on print size, appearance, and pedagogy rather than on content. In line with the recent movement to promote academic excellence, the criteria have now been shifted from appearance to content.

In the 1970s the board focused on "legal compliance" in evaluating textbooks, that is, ensuring that all books on the state list accurately portrayed "the cultural and racial diversity of American society." Lobby groups that appeared before the board were primarily concerned with this issue. From 1979 to 1980, 350 people volunteered between 50 and 100 hours each to examine 4,654 items (both books and audiovisual materials) for demeaning labels or racial stereotypes; equal representation of males and females in occupations, societal contributions, and physical activities; and representation of older and disabled persons. As illustrations began to feature such innovations as women operating jackhammers and steam shovels, the citations against publishers decreased.

Tight schedules and lack of funds to compensate evaluators for their painstaking work were persistent problems. Recruiting volunteers to review for compliance the textbooks displayed at 29 centers around the state was difficult. As board members themselves reviewed textbooks, they had only the most general guidelines to help them distinguish among the books offered—such as exhortations that books be "well written." At first, readability formulas that measure how many difficult words are introduced in each chapter seemed useful, but these are simplistic and sometimes discredited as contributing to reduced academic standards. Because the curricular frameworks were not explicit, the board had to rely on the informed judgments of people working at full-time jobs, who found it difficult to keep up with the adoption-cycle timelines.

Similar problems are to be found nationwide. A member of the North Carolina State Board reported that in one six-week period in

1984 she received 700 books for a single subject area. A reading series by one publisher, designed for all the grades from kindergarten through high school, can have 144 separate pieces, including text, workbooks, teacher's manuals, supplementary audiovisual materials, computer packages, and so on. Some advisers had to resort to the "eight-second thumb test," skimming the pages for appearance—hardly an appropriate process considering the importance of the decision to students, teachers, publishers, and the public. The final rank-order list adopted by the board would exclude some publishers from millions of dollars in sales.

Trends in Textbooks

After I had signed purchase contracts, board member Bill Honig (now the chief state school officer in California) led an inquiry into our results. As we examined the chosen textbooks—with our attention no longer focused on creation science, legal compliance, and procedure—we sadly concluded that many of the books were dull, drained of excitement, and diluted in content. The print was bigger and the pictures more colorful, but the sentences were shorter and the words simpler. Compare the 1971 version of Marshall's discovery of gold in California with its 1980 counterpart:

(1971)

The next morning he shut off the water and walked along beside the millrace, to learn whether the water had cleaned it out. The weather was clear and cold. It was probably January 24, although no one was sure of the exact date.

"My eye was caught with the glimpse of something shining in the bottom of the ditch," Marshall said later. "I reached my hand down and picked it up. It made my heart thump, for I was certain that it was gold."

The piece was round and smaller than a pea. He put it on a flat rock and hammered it. It did not crumble or break. He was sure then that it was metal.

He showed it to the men. He made them promise to keep working until the sawmill was finished. "Then," he said, "we will all go hunting for gold."

As the men worked, they picked up a few more pieces of yellow metal. Marshall put the pieces into a tiny green glass bottle. On January 28 he rode through a hard rainstorm to the fort. He and Sutter went into Sutter's office and locked the door. They shook the yellow flakes from the bottle and weighed them carefully. They were heavy for their size. Gold is very heavy. They put a chemical called nitric acid on the flakes. Nothing happened. Gold will not dissolve in nitric acid.

Now Sutter was sure that Marshall had found gold. They rode back to the mill and asked the workers to keep the discovery a secret. Sutter feared that the men at the fort would leave their jobs to hunt gold if the news spread. Also, he and Marshall wanted time to form a mining company for digging up the gold in the Coloma Valley.[1]

Marshall hired some men to help build the mill. They found a place on the American River where the water ran swiftly. There they built the sawmill. When they put the waterwheel in place, they discovered that it did not turn properly. It was hitting the bottom of the river. They began to remove the dirt at the bottom of the river to make room for the turning wheel. As they worked, James Marshall noticed a shiny nugget on the riverbed. He picked it up.

Back at Sutter's Fort, Marshall and Sutter looked up the article on gold in the American Encyclopedia. They then tested the nugget Marshall had found according to what the article said. In a few hours, they were sure they had discovered gold!

The second passage is shorter by more than 150 words. And while a difficult word ("encyclopedia") does appear, the references to specific ways of testing gold (including the chemical term "nitric acid") have been removed, along with many lively details. Or consider these two descriptions of the San Francisco earthquake of 1906:

(1971)

Just as the sun was rising on the morning of April 18, 1906, the land along the northern part of the San Andreas Fault began to shift. The ground on the west side of the fault moved north. The ground on the east side moved south. Posts that had once stood side by side ended up as much as sixteen feet apart.

Near Santa Cruz, trees five feet thick were broken in two. Buildings collapsed in cities from Santa Rosa in the north to Hollister in the south. Many of the fine new buildings at Stanford University near Palo Alto tumbled to the ground. People were thrown violently off their feet.

The greatest damage was in San Francisco. The ground shivered twice. A grinding noise filled the air. And then, one newspaper report said, there was a "deep roar like heavy surf and a third great shudder ran through the peninsula."

Buildings twisted and fell. There were jangling crashes of glass. Bricks rained into the street, killing men and horses that were pulling delivery wagons. A man who saw the earthquake wrote, "In places the street sank three or four feet. In other places great humps appeared. The streetcar tracks were bent and twisted out of place."[2]

(1980)

San Francisco sits on top of a very long fault called the San Andreas Fault. This fault is more than 1,000 kilometers (650 miles) long. At 5:13 in the morning, April 18, 1906, the San Andreas Fault slipped and shifted. A two-minute earthquake shook San Francisco. Buildings fell apart. Chimneys were knocked over. Water pipes broke. In certain cases, entire buildings fell upon those inside, killing many people.

Gone are "shivered," "shudder," and "jangling." "Buildings collapsed" has become "buildings fell." The new version, one-third the length of the old, is a highly simplified, undramatic description of events. The addition of the fault's length in miles and kilometers is instructive, but it does not compensate the reader for what has been excised and reduced. What had gone wrong?

Kent Gill, chairman of the curriculum commission, reported to the board: "The theory behind the state's multiple adoption system is that it will provide different types of basic textbooks for different types of students. But each publisher is looking at the broad market and feels the slightly easier book reaches a broader market. The whole trend has been to write them slightly below grade level." In addition, Gill said, with money tight, school districts were buying lower-level books accessible to all students in the classroom.

"Publishers simply reflect the attitudes and demands of society," one publisher explained to the *Los Angeles Times* when the board's reaction was reported. The state board's agenda from 1974 to 1979 had been dominated by concerns about the bottom third of the achievement band—the disadvantaged, handicapped, or limited-English-speaking pupils. The publishers had responded to market demand; they were not the cause of the problems. It takes publishers three or four years to develop a new text series for a specific subject, and straying from the middle of the market can be dangerous. The $1.2 billion-a-year industry is very competitive: A half dozen presidents of major educational publishers were replaced in 1981.

To send the market a signal, the California board decided to reverse its policy of adopting 10 to 15 books per subject and to restrict adoptions to 5 to 8 books of "a high standard." Criteria given to bidders became more explicit, favoring "grade-level" materials. But the board had difficulty "narrowing the gate." Some members argued for the widest possible selection of materials to serve the enormous diversity of the state. Leaders of the curriculum commission argued that supplementary materials could be used for above-average students. At last the board asked the curriculum commission to recommend a "balanced matrix," with most books at grade level, but some above or below it. Thus, in the 1983 cycle in history and social sciences, the board adopted 7 books for grade 8; in the previous cycle it had approved 13.

Colliding Influences

Companies whose textbooks were rejected hired lawyers and lobbyists and enlisted the support of satisfied customers from local school districts. The publishers' principal lobbyist had close ties to key legislators, having been chief of legislative relations for the Department of Education. A publisher from a small company personally pressured board members outside meeting rooms and in hotel lobbies. But the board held to its new policy.

In this instance, the board was influenced in its selection of text-books chiefly by the specialists on the curriculum commission, but many other influences entered the process. National policies, shaped by Congress, had directed attention to students in the lower third of the achievement band and to a spectrum of problems arising from racism and sex-role stereotyping. Members of the judiciary played a part by ensuring compliance with national policy. Special interest groups influenced choice by occupying the time and attention of those who had the power to choose. Publishers' practices, responsive to forces of the marketplace, strongly influenced the range of materials from which a selection could be made. State policies established the process of selection. Among all these pressures, none was directed toward setting high standards for the content of these textbooks. While strong pressure groups supported creationism and opposed sex-stereotyping, among the many forces shaping the curriculum no lobby spoke for rigorous and challenging content. Opponents of junk food fought against books that favorably pictured ice cream cones. But no one fought *for* interesting books and *against* dull ones.

Ideally, curriculum development of the type the National Science Foundation sponsored in the 1960s should precede and guide textbook adoption. But after the flap in 1975 over the federally funded series, "Man: A Course of Study" (MACOS)—the curriculum that was met with violence in Kanawha County, West Virginia—Congress eliminated the federal role in curriculum development, and no other agency entered. No single state government has the money to develop new curricula, and there are no interstate mechanisms. Typical of the debate in Congress over MACOS was the charge made by John Conlan (R., Arizona) that it represented a federal attempt to "use classrooms for conditioning, to mold a new generation of Americans toward a repudiation of traditional values, behavior and patriotic beliefs." Twenty years before, the federal government had entered the curriculum and text development field because critics alleged that school-books were outdated, inaccurate, dull, and lacking in diversity. Now the scholars and experts on whom the federal and state governments had relied were being criticized for trying to impose their own cosmopolitan and secular values.

Some publishers and educators contend that the problems of text adoption could be alleviated by abolishing state adoptions. Centralized state control, critics say, invites lobbying by publishers, restricts choice, focuses on sensational issues like creationism, and leads to low-budget evaluation procedures. But the California board was not impressed by the capacity of the local school districts for thorough evaluation of textbooks. Local school boards spent less time on curricular deliberations than the state board did. Nor had local demand in non-adoption states resulted in more challenging books. Teachers, given little or no released time or compensation, could not be expected to analyze texts in detail. These shortcomings were especially acute in small school districts. If the states withdrew, would the big cities merely take their place as the dominant market force?

During the 1970s, text standards had declined. By 1980, centralized leadership seemed necessary to reverse the trend, and in March 1984 23 states met in Florida to discuss interstate cooperation in text buying. Florida governor Bob Graham challenged the conferees to form a buyers' "cartel for excellence." Chief state school officers across the country and the National Association of State Boards of Education are now working to carry out this plan.

But I remain intrigued by the possibilities of decentralized text adoptions. The cartel of state buyers will further erode local discretion to choose textbooks. But local choice can mean little without careful review of books. Perhaps the national interest in master or mentor teachers will create a cadre of evaluators. Certainly, classroom teachers and local curricular specialists would have to spend many hours at the task. The best text adoption system remains undiscovered, but one thing is certain: Policymakers must pay more attention to this critical issue.

Case Study in Policy Making: The New Math Movement

The two-decade effort, beginning in the mid-1950s, to introduce a new math curriculum illustrates professional control at its best and also reveals the limits of professional power. The care with which the new curriculum was systematically developed and introduced is a model of professional technique, yet this major curricular change, introduced step by step throughout all levels of education, did not endure.

The traditional methods of teaching mathematics in public schools are rooted in early nineteenth-century pedagogy. For some time mathematicians and school math teachers had been discontented with these methods. During the early 1950s, this discontent was sufficient to generate only a scattered questioning of the old ways. Some university professors were experimenting with a new approach to math instruction, but there was no national sense of urgency, nor were resources committed to any plan of action.

Then, following the shock that accompanied the Russian success in orbiting the first space vehicle, what had been a professional issue was transformed into a public issue. Critics of American schools who were already charging educators with training the modern generation poorly seized on Sputnik as evidence, attributing this American "defeat" to "poor" schools. Thus an external technological event provided interested groups with an opportunity to press for curricular improvements, particularly in language and mathematics training. The media appealed to university curriculum specialists for enlightenment; parents demanded action of state and national policymakers, and the question was quickly placed on the political agenda.

To provide students with better math training became national policy. Congress legislated and the U.S. Office of Education implemented a law providing funds to improve the quality of math and language training and to increase the supply of teachers in these subjects. This National Defense Education Act (NDEA) of 1958 provided funds for developing new curricula in math, training currently employed teachers in the new math, and incorporating training in the new math into the curriculum of schools of education.

The next stage, implementation, was impressive in its thoroughness. Federal agencies fastened on a particular strategy for raising students' math comprehension. This involved a new way of thinking about math theoretically, an approach that could be taught from the first grade onward and by methods students could easily grasp. The traditional curriculum ladder (arithmetic, geometry, beginning and advanced algebra, trigonometry, and—in some schools—calculus) was abandoned almost everywhere. Instead, students were introduced sequentially to different levels and to relevant applications of such concepts as set theory. Thus, to get across the concept of numbering, instead of using the traditional method of counting from the base of ten, students were taught to count from the base of seven or another number. Comprehension of the logic of numbering was sought rather than the rote learning of a multiplication table.

Federal funds underwrote eight- to ten-week summer training institutes for many teachers under the leadership of the National Science Foundation (NSF). Special text materials were devised and disseminated; later, computer applications became available. States endorsed these innovations, providing additional funds to incorporate the new into the old math curriculum. State administrative agencies enlarged their curriculum divisions relevant to math programs and assisted in the implementation of the changes. Local school boards participated by releasing their teachers for summer instruction. If one's school system did not enjoy the new math, one felt left out of a national tide of change. Retraining and materials were provided for every level of schooling, and public and parochial schools alike were enlisted in moving the reform into the system and onto the students. This was all done in a remarkably few years (1958-66).

The New Math Movement: Reaction

The program began to produce results, among them one that was unintended. If a major goal of the program was to improve math training, then millions of students had been exposed to the new math concepts and understood them reasonably well. If another goal was to institutionalize the reform, then thousands of school districts had adopted the new curricular concept. But if the goal was to prepare students for the application of mathematics to life, some of the feedback was strongly negative. Parents increasingly complained that their children could not use mathematics for everyday requirements such as multiplying or adding in preparing a bill or grocery list. Parents themselves often did not understand the new math concepts despite efforts by educators to give them a quick introduction.

It was not easy to monitor whether teachers stressed the new math. There was little evidence that students were learning mathematical principles any better. Indeed, given the widespread decline in math (and English) test scores across the nation in the mid-1970s, few curricula could claim much success. The negative feedback became so widespread that by the 1970s state laws and regulations were altered. State text adoptions returned to the old math, and state tests changed accordingly. Teachers, too, were reverting to the old math. Some continued to use their new-math skills gained through NSF summer institutes, but hostile external forces gradually diminished individual commitment. The new math had no strong constituency within the school system to counter the reaction, and no support from any lobby other than leaders in the federal government operating through the NSF. Unlike vocational education or driver's training, it had not stimulated the growth of a separate department or group of specialized teachers.

By the mid-1970s, the feedback cycle had resulted in a full turn away from the new curriculum, and little remained of what had been an aggressive national effort. The national government could stimulate change in the mathematics curriculum but could not sustain it without a commitment from those at the local level. The rise and fall of the new math illustrates the potential—and limits—of centralized control in an educational system with a tradition of local and classroom discretion. It demonstrates that parents and citizens can control school policy and reject unacceptable federal or state policies.

Trends in School Governance

The dispute over centralized control of the schools really revolves about three traditional values: equal treatment, freedom of choice, and efficiency or effectiveness. The rationale for state intervention is sound: Only the state can ensure equality and standardization of instruction and resources. But the rationale for local control is also sound. Local control assures that programs work efficiently and effectively where they must—in particular classrooms, with particular students. And through freedom of choice, local control ensures commitment to programs on the part of those who implement them.

In the 1970s the demand for equal educational opportunity spawned new state programs for populations with special needs. States now classify children and mandate services and standards for many categories of students: the mentally gifted, the disadvantaged, migrants, underachievers, the non-English-speaking, American Indians, pregnant minors, foster children, delinquent children, and 20 or more categories of handicapped children. By 1981 bilingual education statutes regulated local teaching policy in 24 states. In California, for example, any class with ten or more pupils whose English is limited must have a state-specified program. Federal programs for the disadvantaged and handicapped require the states to impose additional requirements on local schools and to determine whether a local proposal meets federal regulations. Sixteen states, building on the federal concept, have started their own programs for the disadvantaged. In the 1970s, states have been suspicious that local commitment to disadvantaged and minority populations would be inadequate without state regulations to ensure equal access and equal treatment.

State governments, skeptical, too, of local willingness to adopt innovative programs, have initiated such programs, for which localities may compete. Several states have plans to develop high schools for selected specialties, such as science or the performing arts. California has developed the School Improvement Program, which provides over $100 per pupil to be spent at the discretion of school-based councils composed of parents, teachers, administrators, and students. These school-site councils are charged with devising new ways to individualize education. To provide greater local flexibility, some states, for example, have adopted legislation to permit lawyers, craftspeople, and artists to teach courses, even though they lack formal teaching credentials. In addition, some states permit waivers of state requirements if the local district can provide justification.

Another development has been state mandating of "accountability." Traditionally, states have defined minimum requirements, such as number of days of instruction. Accountability, in contrast, has focused state control on educational outcomes, such as measurable levels of student achievement. Between 1966 and 1976, 35 states passed accountability statutes. In Florida, for example, to obtain a high school diploma, students must score in the 70th percentile on statewide tests. Test scores are then used to evaluate schools, teachers, and programs. School districts fear the adverse publicity that can come with publication of test scores lower than those of other districts.

The 1983-84 "Crisis": The States React

According to the national reports of 1983-84, local school officials caused the current crisis in education by allowing academic standards to drop; they "unilaterally educationally disarmed" the nation. State legislators have been told that the federal government will not play a major role in funding responses to this crisis. State reaction has been intense and pervasive. The 1983-84 meetings of the National Governors Association were dominated by issues of education reform. State legislative agendas are replete with six- or eight-point plans by major state authorities for educational improvement. Statewide business groups have formed task forces for state action. With over 200 high-level state commissions studying the quality of education in 1983-84, it is not unusual for the state legislature, the governor, and the chief state school officers to have separate commissions.

The trend in state/local relations is strikingly clear: The states are seizing the initiative, while the local school organizations and professional educational organizations are reacting with suggestions for marginal change. This acceleration of state activity, focusing on curricular standards and teaching quality, promises to restructure state/local relations, especially when added to the 1970-80 growth in state control, focusing on school finance reform, categorical programs, school improvement, minimum competency, and civil rights regulations. Though some states, such as New Hampshire, are not active, the following summary illustrates the scope and intensity of state intervention:

> • Florida enacted a $425 million increase in funding for education and instituted merit pay, graduation requirements, improved math/science programs, and higher academic standards.
>
> • California enacted 80 reforms, encompassing mentor teachers, an achievement exam for seniors based on the New York Regents exam, fiscal incentives for lengthened school days, increased salaries for beginning teachers, and revised criteria for discipline.
>
> • Illinois raised income and sales taxes to fund support for stricter graduation standards and fiscal incentives for programs serving gifted students; it also instituted mandatory collective bargaining for teachers.
>
> • Tennessee, Arkansas, and 16 other states are revising their teacher evaluation, certification, and pay policies, including development of career ladders for teachers.
>
> • Over 30 states have increased requirements for admission to their public universities by stressing heavier academic loads for high school juniors and seniors.
>
> • Thirty-five states have increased high school graduation standards.
>
> • Sixteen states have initiated a longer school day or year.

The new state initiatives are aimed at the core of instructional policy: what should be taught, how it should be taught, and who shall teach. State reformers no longer want to stop at the classroom door. They

"What did I learn today? My mother will want to know."

believe they must influence the content and style of instruction within that classroom if reforms are to take root. But state regulations cannot easily be adapted to diverse local school contexts. There is a contradiction between state policies designed to attract and retain high-quality teachers and state minimum standards for classroom coverage of a particular subject. Teachers are attracted to the opportunity to exercise independence and creativity, but not to demands that they cover subject matter as directed by state regulations and align instruction with items on statewide tests.

To move local schools toward higher academic standards the state canot rely solely upon curricular mandates and tests. An increase in time spent on homework, for example, is best encouraged by providing support services for teachers rather than by mandating two hours of homework a night. An aggressive state stance on these issues raises the difficult question of state versus local control.

There is no counterforce to this growth of central control. The states are playing a leadership role in 1983 because of a striking lack of countervailing initiative and power at the local or professional level. Local school boards, administrators, teachers, PTAs, and taxpayers are either forced or content to play a reactive role. School boards and administrators have the means, through their statewide organizations, to devise their own plans for raising academic standards and for presenting such plans to the state policymakers. I find it surprising that so few have done this.

Although dominant political and social forces are moving toward ever more court and state intervention in local policy making, local control is still a cherished principle. To ignore its political importance is to risk a pendulum swing of reaction. A wise leadership—state or national—would recommend pruning state education codes to maintain equilibrium between state and local control. Regulation in curricular areas, for example, might be offset by lifting some of the detailed prescriptions concerning specific practices within the classroom. The state code could eliminate at least some traditional regulations requiring expenditure of large amounts of money. To illustrate, 31 states now have statutes requiring some form of contractual agreement between school systems and employees. But this state mandate to bargain collectively has not been accompanied by repeal of personnel restrictions written into earlier state codes. Because states continue to set standards for personnel much as they did before teachers were permitted to bargain with local school boards, unions have the advantage of starting from a guaranteed base built into the state code.

Needed Changes in Governance: A Utopian View

In the current environment of education, something needs to be done to reinvigorate local control. The new priorities should be decentralization, increased representation, and lay control. The best federal and state policy for the present would be to provide the resources and stimulation that would encourage major decisions at the school site. The value conflicts inherent in education should be highlighted, not obscured behind a façade of professional expertise, or lost among the corridors of fragmented authority.

In the past, local control has supported retrograde policies leading to discrimination against racial minorities and women, and in the neglect of handicapped and low-achieving students. But federal and state legislation has effectively put an end to these practices. Similarly, the states have gone a long way toward eliminating inequities arising from traditional ways of financing education. These reforms were needed. For the most part, they are now in place and will continue in force. Without losing these gains in equality, education policy could now turn to another set of concerns, primarily the concerns for the quality of education voiced in the 1983 reports.

One idea of particular promise is the California School Improvement Program (SIP), which is designed to improve the quality of public education by stimulating change on a school site basis. The program has few requirements except that each school (1) initiate an organized effort to identify the strengths and weaknesses of its education program; (2) plan activities that build on strengths and respond to weaknesses; (3) evaluate the results of these efforts; and (4) modify things that are not working.

A council composed equally of educators, parents or community members, and, at the secondary level, students, is formed in every participating school. Unlike the various categorical programs, each with a separate advisory group composed of advocates for the special needs of a particular class of students, the School Improvement Program serves the entire student population. Its council binds together the interests of parents and community members in examining the quality of the school's program for all students. Teachers might form a faculty senate at each school as they did in San Jose, California, to elect representatives to the school site council. Such an organization

AS TEACHERS REQUESTED IT

AS PRINCIPALS ORDERED IT

AS CENTRAL OFFICE DESIGNED IT

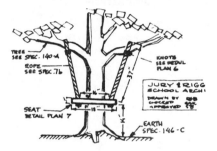

TREE
SEE SPEC. 140-A

ROPE
SEE SPEC. 7b

SEAT
DETAIL PLAN 7

KNOTS
SEE DETAIL
PLAN 6

JURY & RIGG
SCHOOL ARCHI
DRAWN BY
CHECKED
APPROVED

EARTH
SPEC. 146-C

AS BOARD OF EDUCATION APPROVED IT

AS MAINTENANCE INSTALLED IT

WHAT THE STUDENTS WANTED

would help overcome the isolation of teachers that has impeded co-operative school planning.

Qualifying schools receive approximately $120 per pupil in state funds to use as the planning council sees fit. The state requires no uniform plan or procedure. The Department of Education has consistently emphasized that when a plan is not working to achieve the council's objectives, it should be changed. A plan, then, is not an instrument of centralized statewide regulation, but a framework within which schools and districts can organize their programs and design improvements. The funding provided under SIP is wholly discretionary. There are no particular expenditures that must be made under the program. Schools are free to take risks and to buy materials and services not otherwise available, or, if a school feels it has a good program, to reinforce that program rather than change it.

The SIP idea has spread across about 3,400 California schools. Currently it serves 1.36 million children and costs the state about $188 million a year. It is an impressive example of the state's willingness to support and trust local discretion.

The SIP style of governance could be strengthened and used widely. In a more encompassing form, school-site decision making would be preceded by a complete overhaul and pruning of the state education code to permit more local options. Then each school would elect a citizen-staff council similar to those in SIP. In place of the minuscule amount of discretionary funds made available under SIP, large amounts of state and local unrestricted funds would be allocated to each school to spend as it chose. The school council would decide the instructional priorities (how much time for basics) and school organization (open or traditional classrooms).

Many activities would remain centralized. Policies governing equal access and equal treatment would continue to be controlled by state or federal authorities and enforced by the courts. Collective bargaining with teachers would continue at the district level—because if individual school decision making were viewed as a device to undermine teachers' rights and collective bargaining, it would surely fail. Other decisions would be reviewed by central authorities. For example, the council might recommend to the central authorities the retention or replacement of the principal at the end of a three- to five-year contract. On the other hand, some issues now decided centrally would be reserved for the school-site council. For example, with the core curriculum fixed, the council could use its discretion as to secondary school electives. Or, a council could vary the pattern of school staffing by hiring fewer teachers and more counselors, or fewer teachers and more teacher's aides.

Strengthening the School Board

This new focus on the individual school would be accompanied by a strengthening of the central school board. The school board would continue to make broad policy decisions, while educators at each school site, guided by the views of parents, would have greater control over that school's budget, staff, and curriculum.

To strengthen school boards would mean changing current practices in school board elections. Such reforms might begin with the following steps:

1. School board elections should take place in subcommunity districts rather than at large.

2. All candidates for membership on a school board should run at one time. In this way the public could vote for significant policy changes rather than electing a few new members each year. In large districts, school board members should receive salaries and should surrender part of their outside activities.

3. Partisan endorsements should be allowed (though not required) to give voters more clues as to the philosophies of candidates.

4. To enhance effectiveness, school boards should have their own independent staffs.

Some states—Florida is one—have discovered that school-site decision making requires preparation of principals, teachers, and parents. The central school district would have the major role in conducting such training along with responsibility for evaluation and oversight. At the high school level there might also be need for district-wide coordination of work-study, off-campus programs, and so on. The present profusion of overlapping and uncoordinated parent advisory groups mandated by federal or state law could largely be eliminated, if each school had a council at the school site.

Each school would prepare an annual report of school performance. This would cover the nature of the school's objectives; a de-

TABLE 7-2

Expenditure Variations among Elementary Schools in the Newport-Mesa Unified School District, 1972–73

Expenditure Category	Average District-wide Expenditure per Pupil	School-by-School Variation in Expenditure per Pupil
Health Supplies	$ 0.10	$ 0.00 – $ 0.26
Textbooks	0.15	0.00 – 1.24
Professional Meetings	0.16	0.00 – 1.56
Other Books	0.74	0.00 – 1.74
Office Supplies	1.00	0.00 – 2.59
Field Trips	1.15	0.32 – 2.58
Telephone	1.49	0.90 – 2.36
New Equipment	3.02	0.07 – 11.07
Instructional Supplies	13.35	8.25 – 33.68

Source: Walter I. Garms, James W. Guthrie, Lawrence C. Pierce, *School Finance: The Economics and Politics of Public Education* (Englewood Cliffs, N.J.: Prentice-Hall, 1978).

In this district some parts of the school budget are set at the school site; each school has a larger budget in discretionary funds than is usually the case. Under this system, schools diverge widely in their spending patterns.

scription of the teachers, students, and programs; and a display of educational outcomes such as students' test scores, number of drop-outs, and curriculum coverage. The principal would evaluate the goals, strengths, and weaknesses of the existing program, and would present as part of the report a five-year plan incorporating approaches for correcting identified weaknesses. Reports on the school-site perfor-mance would be mailed to each parent and sent to community news-papers and to all community groups. The school council would play a major role in preparing this report.

This type of governance plan recognizes the school rather than the entire district or state as the critical nexus between the child and the substance of education. Even if community participation were not high at all school sites, this plan would still have beneficial effects. In addition to *what* is done in governance, *how* things are done and how people feel about their governance is crucial to successful and enduring policy.

There is, of course, no one best system of school governance, and various localities might use different forms. Newport-Mesa school district in California has a small-scale version of the system of school-site governance I have just outlined. There, it results in a marked variation in funding patterns: Some schools stress more books, others more counselors (see Table 7-2).

With safeguards to prevent racial and economic segregation, an emphasis on the school site can be linked to parental choice. Schools in the same geographical area could feature quite different programmatic approaches, and parents could choose the one they prefer. As choices are opened to parents, they can exert greater leverage over school policy, even economic leverage—schools in which enrollment declined could lose part of their funding.

Flexibility is one of the chief advantages of local control. Within one elementary school district in Florida, I found a wide range among students scoring poorly on tests—from 22 percent in one school to 78 percent in another. Such diversity in skill levels requires an equal diversity in the practices, programs, and instructional methods of schools. As Theodore Sizer argues, flexibility can also lead to improving the school curriculum:

> Personalization of learning and instruction requires a flexible structure. A flexible structure implies a *simple structure*. A school day segmented into seven or eight times, each with its own set of imperatives, is almost impossible to bend. A curriculum represented by six or seven autonomous subjects quickly freezes hard: if each gets what its teacher feels is its due, all lose substantial freedom. Furthermore, such a fractionated and specialized set of subjects distorts knowledge for young minds; a simpler, more cogent organization of subject matter is wise.[3]

While a central authority, political or professional, might design a coherent and cogent curriculum, a local council, working with parents, students, and teachers, has the best chance of implementing one.

Even without councils at school sites, one kind of local control remains potent. America's more than two million public school teachers have in effect a pocket veto on what is taught. An old tradition in American public schools is that once the door of the classroom shuts nobody checks on what a teacher actually does. So long as teachers consider themselves professional agents with some autonomy in curriculum questions by virtue of their professional expertise, policy implementation will be a matter of persuasion rather than direction.

CHAPTER

RENEWING THE TEACHING PROFESSION

The success of an educational system inevitably depends upon the judgment and ability of those who teach—the rest of the educational apparatus is "overhead." It is in the classroom that the pupil experiences the educational process; if the interaction between teacher and child is not effective, even the most sound federal, state, or local policies will be useless. Reducing objectives for the schools and revamping the curriculum will improve public education only if teachers are of high quality.

Economically, too, teachers are the critical component of the system. About 85 percent of all salaries in education go to teachers—65 percent of the total budget. To be productive and, in a sense, to invest public funds wisely, schools must recruit, retain, and reward a corps of competent professionals, imbued with high standards of performance and capable of commanding the respect of their "clients"—their pupils, the parents, and the public.

In 1983 "declining teacher quality" suddenly became an issue for the American media. Every national commission report highlights the problems of the teaching profession and calls for drastic change. A number of negative trends affecting the profession are often mentioned; low pay, declining prestige, decreasing academic ability among the teachers themselves, poor working conditions, inadequate training, and low rates of retention are among the troubling complaints.[1] Yet why so much concern now? After all, these problems, which result from an interrelated set of historical circumstances, have been building for years.

TABLE 8-1

Enrollment in Public Elementary and Secondary Schools, 1968-90

Year	K-12 Total	K-8	9-12
	(in millions)		
1968	44.9	32.2	12.7
1971	46.1	32.3	13.8
1974	45.1	30.9	14.1
1977	43.6	29.3	14.2
1980[a]	41.0	27.7	13.3
1983[b]	39.2	27.0	12.1
1986	39.5	27.4	12.1
1990	41.3	30.2	11.0

[a] Based on estimates.
[b] Figures for 1983, 1986, and 1990 are projected.

Sources: Department of Education, National Center for Education Statistics, *Projections of Education Statistics to 1988-89* (Washington, D.C.: U.S. Government Printing Office, 1981) and *Projections of Education Statistics to 1990-91* (Washington, D.C.: U.S. Government Printing Office, 1982).

After declining over the past decade, school enrollment will increase by 2 million from 1985 to 1990.

One reason for the present intense scrutiny of the teaching profession is that trends in student enrollment are changing once again. After declining over the past decade, enrollment will increase by 2 million from 1985 to 1990 (see Table 8-1). Moreover, from 1970 to 1982 very few new teachers were hired, so that the average teacher is older and is close to retirement. Nationally, we must soon begin hiring more teachers (see Table 8-2). In the eighties, teaching will be one of the fastest growing professions. The student population is changing as well as growing; these new teachers will confront a higher proportion of pupils from disadvantaged and single-parent homes. By 1990 about two-thirds of the national student population will come from such households.

There is an even more significant reason for looking closely at the teaching profession: fundamental changes in the labor market for teachers. Taken together, the circumstances surrounding the work force in education compel a rethinking of the very concept of the teaching profession.

The Changing Labor Market

Women make up two-thirds of the total work force of teachers—and 80 percent of all elementary school teachers. The dependence of the teaching profession on women is a major cause for concern, be-

TABLE 8-2

Estimated Supply of Teachers Compared with
Estimated Demand for Additional Teachers

Year	Estimated Supply of New Teachers	Estimated Demand for Additional Teachers	Supply of New Teachers as a Percentage of Demand for Additional Teachers
1969-73	1,492,000	990,000	150.7%
1974-78	1,132,000	819,000	138.2
1979-83	893,000	622,000	143.6
1984-88	780,000	861,000	90.6

Sources: Department of Education, National Center for Education Statistics, *The Condition of Education* (Washington, D.C.: U.S. Government Printing Office, 1980); National Education Association, *Teacher Supply and Demand in Public Schools* (Washington, D.C.: National Education Association of the U.S., 1973, 1977, 1978); Department of Education, National Center for Education Statistics, *Projection of Education Statistics to 1988-89* (Washington, D.C.: U.S. Government Printing Office, 1980).

If the teaching profession can attract young candidates, a resurgence of demand for teachers will make it one of the fastest-growing professions of the late 1980s.

cause the vast expansion of occupational choices for young women has correspondingly decreased the supply of superior teachers. Women who achieve high scores on academic tests have disappeared from the school employers' personnel files over the past 15 years because teaching—like nursing, librarianship, and social work—is no longer one of the few places for them to go. Management, law, medicine—all the opportunities are open to them today. The bright young woman who taught English 15 years ago is now carrying an attaché case and heading for an office. The statistics bear this out. In North Carolina, for example, the proportion of men scoring well on the National Teacher Exam has remained fairly stable, but the proportion of women scoring well has dropped sharply. In 1966, for every three women who majored in business, nine majored in education. Only 11 years later, for every three women who majored in business, four majored in education. Thus, in a single year (1977), more than 100,000 women were lost to education. To put it bluntly, sexism once helped preserve quality in the public schools.

The expansion in employment opportunities has also enabled racial minorities to move into occupations formerly closed to them, so that the same pattern occurs: In 1983 the number of black teacher candidates in the Southeast who could pass a state screening test of basic skills dropped alarmingly. In Alabama, 51 percent failed, and in Arkansas, 47 percent.

New opportunities for women affect teacher quality in another way. Women who withdrew from teaching to raise families once constituted a vast reserve army of teachers who could be called upon as their children grew up. But today, about 70 percent of women between the ages of 25 and 65 are already employed, meaning that the reserve army no longer exists. Education must compete on its own merits as a desirable occupation. But can it do that? Some disturbing recent signs are sketched below.

Disturbing Indicators

An important reason for the decline in teacher quality is the nature of the job itself. Talented persons are not likely to choose a career that restricts them to an environment that is (or is perceived to be) stressful and sometimes violent. In addition, public school teaching is now considered low-status among the college educated who are potential teachers or the parents of potential teachers. According to some evidence, public school teaching has lost more occupational prestige in the past 15 to 20 years than any other occupation ranked in the polls.[2]

Fewer and fewer college undergraduates want to be educators. Together with enhanced opportunities and the diminished attractiveness of the profession, a shrinking number of teaching jobs available during the 1970s has brought about a precipitous decline. Whereas in 1970 almost 20 percent of college freshmen expressed an interest in becoming teachers, now only 4.7 percent are so inclined. The percentages are dramatically lower at intensively selective institutions. At the University of California at Berkeley, an institution that supplies more volunteers for altruistic endeavors such as the Peace Corps and Vista than any other campus in the United States, fewer than .01 percent of entering freshmen express an interest in elementary or secondary education as a career.

One explanation for the diminished attractiveness of education as a career is the substantial erosion of public respect and support for teachers. Whatever education formerly lacked in prestige was at least partially offset by the prospect of secure and dignified employment. But teacher layoffs, inflation-ravaged salaries, school closures, and highly publicized strikes have tarnished this aura. Parents are now discouraging their children from becoming teachers. A 1983 Gallup poll reveals that only 45 percent of parents polled thought teaching a

TABLE 8-3

Average Annual Salary of Teachers in Public Schools, 1929–81

Year	Teachers' Salaries (unadjusted dollars)	Teachers' Salaries (adjusted dollars)[a]
1929-30	$ 1,420	$ 5,547
1939-40	1,441	7,063
1949-50	3,010	8,708
1959-60	5,174	11,547
1969-70	8,840	16,035
1975-76	13,155[b]	16,248[b]
1978-79	15,615[b]	15,615[b]
1980-81	18,409[b]	14,075[b]

[a] Represents 1978-79 purchasing power based on the consumer price index, prepared by the Bureau of Labor Statistics, Department of Labor.
[b] Based on estimates.

Sources: Department of Education, National Center for Education Statistics, *Digest of Education Statistics* (Washington, D.C.: U.S. Government Printing Office, 1980), *Statistics of State School Systems* (Washington, D.C.: U.S. Government Printing Office, various years), and National Education Association, *Estimates of School Statistics* (Washington, D.C.: National Education Association of the U.S., 1978-79).

The purchasing power of the average annual salary for teachers peaked in 1972-73 but declined thereafter.

desirable career for their children. Contrast this with the 75 percent who believed, only 14 years ago, that teaching was a good calling.

Despite having to swim upstream against peer and parent pressure, some undergraduates still decide to pursue teacher training. Regrettably, when compared to applicants for professional training in business, science, medicine, and law, education students have low grades and dismal Scholastic Aptitude Test (SAT) and Graduate Record Examination (GRE) scores. Philip Schlechty at the University of North Carolina reports the following for the United States: Teachers-in-training ranked fourteenth out of 16 occupational groupings on SAT verbal scores and fifteenth out of 16 on quantitative scores. Teacher trainees' SAT scores were 52 points below the national average on the test's quantitative dimension. Teacher trainee SAT scores have declined more rapidly over the last decade than has the national average, and their grade-point averages are low when compared to grades of students in professional programs.

Another disturbing sign has been the absolute and relative decline in teachers' salaries (see Tables 8-3 and 8-4). Gary Sykes of Stanford has produced a number of comparisons:

In absolute terms the purchasing power of the average annual salary for teachers peaked in 1972-73 but declined thereafter; by 1979-80 the average teacher had lost more than $1,000 in real purchasing power. To take another measure, the ratio of average teacher salary to the "intermediate family budget" (as set forth by the Department of Labor) declined steadily from its high point of 88.9% in 1972-73 to 78% in 1979-80. Likewise, a recent study comparing teachers' salaries with those of all production workers and specifically with steelworkers and auto workers found that differentials had shrunk steadily through the seventies so that the salary advantage that teachers enjoyed in the early seventies had disappeared by 1978. Even in comparison to other full-time state and local government employees, teachers' salary advantage had shrunk from 25% in 1971 to 19.5% in 1978.[3]

Yet this overall decline is but one part of the problem. The salary scale of teachers is an issue in itself, usually one discussed under the heading of the "career ladder." On the typical salary schedule, a teacher's salary peaks after 12 years. After that, only cost-of-living raises are provided at best. What this means is that the top lifetime salary of a career teacher, however gifted, energetic, and dedicated to the profession, is about $30,000 in a high-cost-of-living area like San Francisco. To go beyond that, a teacher must be promoted out of the

TABLE 8-4

Teachers' Salaries as Compared to Average Salaries in All Industries

Year	Elementary and Secondary Teachers' Salaries	Average Salaries of Full-Time Employees in All Industries	Percent Above Average Received by Teachers
1929-30	$ 1,420	$ 1,386	2.4%
1939-40	1,441	1,282	12.4
1949-50	3,010	2,930	2.7
1959-60	5,174	4,632	11.7
1969-70	8,840	7,334	20.5
1975-76	13,120	11,218	16.9
1980-81	18,409	16,050	14.7

Source: National Center for Education Statistics, Digest of Education Statistics (Washington, D.C.: U.S. Government Printing Office, 1982), p. 57.

Salaries of production workers have been gaining on salaries of teachers.

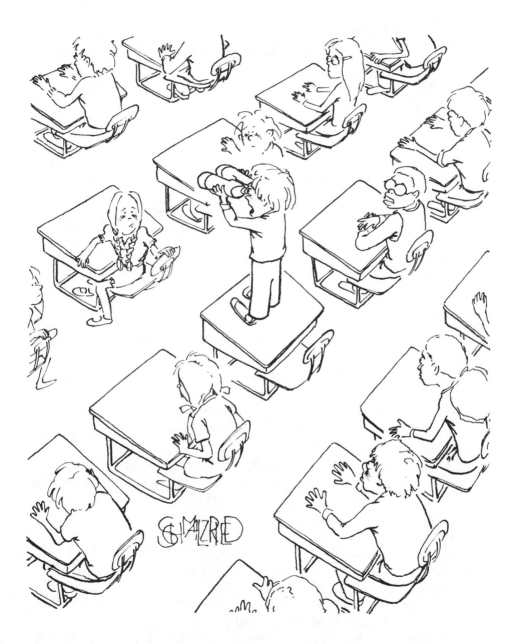

"I . . . think I can make out the teacher!"

TABLE 8-5

Tennessee Teachers' Pay Scales

Traditional Pay Scale (10 months)

Years	0	1	2	3	4	5	6	7
Bachelor's Degree	12,130	12,310	12,495	12,680	12,860	13,030	13,210	13,395
	8	9	10	11	12	13	13	15
	13,560	13,730	13,905	14,095	14,275	14,450	14,625	14,810
Years	0	1	2	3	4	5	6	7
Master's Degree	13,220	13,425	13,625	13,820	14,010	14,210	14,405	14,610
	8	9	10	11	12	13	13	15
	14,810	15,000	15,190	15,390	15,580	15,780	15,985	16,185

Career Ladder Incentive Pay Scale

	(10 months)			(11 months)		(12 months)
Year	4	9	13	9	13	13
Bachelor's Degree	13,860	14,860	15,860	17,730	19,450	21,450
Master's Degree	14,010	17,000	18,780	19,000	20,780	22,780

Career ladders pay teachers more for performing *different duties* than their colleagues. In Tennessee, the career ladder comprises three ranks: professional, senior teacher, and master teacher. The higher ranks have special duties, such as supervising new teachers or planning curriculum, some of which can extend the work year from 10 months to 11 or 12 months.

classroom and into education administration. Thus, the most talented and successful teachers are most likely to stop teaching. Instead of working with students, they will work with other administrators and their supporting staffs. Needless to say, teachers themselves have no personal staff support.

The distinction between the career ladder concept, which I support, and merit pay is important. Career ladders pay teachers more for performing *different duties* from those of their colleagues (see Table 8-5). Merit pay rewards teachers with more money for doing the *same job better* than their colleagues. Merit pay, although it has been proposed many times in this decade, has never spread beyond a handful of districts. A basic problem in the granting of pay for "merit" is the difficulty of evaluating which of two good teachers is better, or which among a group of excellent teachers is best. Most merit pay schemes provide salary increments for 5 to 10 percent of teachers.

It is unfair to judge teachers merely by a test. Mastery of subject matter and child development might be criteria for advancement under a merit plan, but teaching requires classroom technique and skill that cannot be judged by answers on paper. Experienced educators need but a few observations of teachers' classes to separate out incompetent teachers from adequate teachers; they have techniques for this. But to make distinctions among several outstanding candidates requires many periods of observation, and the techniques for this complex task are only now being refined. Also, a classroom observer changes the dynamic in a classroom even if the observer is present for only a brief period. In order to grasp the normal pupil-teacher interactions the observer must be more than an occasional special visitor.

Teachers' organizations prefer career ladder plans, such as Tennessee's, to merit pay because more teachers can benefit. Teachers' organizations are also correctly concerned that because the observation of teaching skills on which merit pay would depend is still an underdeveloped science, judgment could be subjective and arbitrary. Unfortunately, very few school principals have ever been required to conduct frequent sessions of observation in order to judge among highly effective teachers, nor are they trained to do so. They have focused their efforts on weeding out gross incompetence.

Negative Working Conditions

Under the present circumstances, teaching lacks the upward pull of a truly professional career in which, as we Americans believe it should, hard work leads to recognition and reward. At age 35, most teachers must look ahead to a lifetime in the classroom with little change in duties and little gain in income. Furthermore, during this lifetime they will be on public view. It is difficult to calculate the consequences of unattractive working conditions. Perhaps if other functions affecting their jobs were altered, teachers could more easily tolerate cramped and inconvenient working conditions. In Japan, for example, teachers often do not have comfortable spaces in which to prepare for and conduct instruction, but they are generally accorded greater public respect. In the United States, however, the overall low regard for teachers appears to be reflected in the lack of privacy accorded them, and in the poor state of repair typical of many schools. Teachers often do not have access even to lunchtime privacy, a shared telephone, or a place to prepare lessons in quiet.

It is not only the physical environment that hampers effective instruction; there is, as we have seen, an astounding array of activities to compete with academic instruction: band and orchestra rehearsals, pep rallies, drama workshops, senior class photos, field trips, student council elections, bloodmobile visits, class meetings, guidance counselor appointments, SAT administration, athletic practice—on and on they go, creating a staggering stream of school-sanctioned classroom interruptions. As important as many of these non-academic activities may be, they nevertheless detract from the prime purpose of schooling. An interruption can so change the atmosphere in a classroom or so fracture the logic of an explanatory sequence that whatever came before the interruption as well as what was to come after is lost. Also, the ease with which teaching can be "bumped" by other activities contributes to the dilution of a legitimate learning environment. The critical component in education—classroom contact between student and teacher—is sometimes treated all too casually.

These conditions are not necessarily the result of public neglect; and they are subject to change by joint action of administrators and teachers. If education is to be accorded professional status and to become an attractive undertaking, then both the physical and psychological environment must provide more support to the teacher.

Negative Results

When queried, a staggering 36 percent of teachers responded that they probably or certainly would not again select teaching as a career. A profession that lacks confidence in itself cannot easily inspire the confidence of others. Table 8-6 reveals some of the reasons for widespread dissatisfaction among teachers. Teachers receive little public respect, are dissatisfied with their university preparation, contend their salaries are too low, and believe they spend too much time on administration. Many of them love to teach and feel that good performance is recognized, but all of these negative factors help cause an alarming rate of teacher turnover.

About one-half leave the profession within their first five to seven years. For the majority of the newly hired, it is more like a procession than a profession. Researchers in North Carolina have found that the teachers earning higher scores on the National Teachers Exam are almost twice as likely to leave teaching than all others who have been teaching the same length of time. Consequently, the talent pool is thinned drastically at the point where long-term career decisions are made.

Educators are also concerned about the increased percentage of teachers prepared at less selective academic institutions.[4] Several prestigious schools, among them Reed, Yale, Harvard, and Duke, dropped

TABLE 8-6

Teachers and Job Satisfaction

	Agree Strongly	Agree Somewhat	Disagree Somewhat	Disagree Strongly	Not Sure
I love to teach.	78%	18%	3%	*	*
I have to spend too much time on administrative tasks.	38%	34%	19%	7%	*
I am usually recognized for good performance.	33%	37%	29%	10%	*
I would advise a young person to pursue a career in teaching.	12%	33%	29%	24%	1%
As a teacher, I feel respected in today's society.	10%	37%	31%	21%	*
The training and preparation teachers receive today does a good job preparing them for the classroom.	10%	36%	31%	19%	3%
My job allows me the opportunity to earn a decent salary.	8%	29%	26%	37%	*

* Less than 0.5%.

Source: Louis Harris and Associates, National Survey of the American Teacher, sponsored by the Metropolitan Life Insurance Company, June 1984; 1,981 respondents.

Problems of the profession as teachers see them: poor salaries, lack of respect, and irrelevant training. Advantages? Teaching itself.

their teacher training programs in the 1970s. In California, the University of California system has only small-scale programs compared to those at the state college and university campuses at San Jose, Fullerton, or Long Beach. In addition, teacher education at any institution of higher education is allotted a much lower expenditure per pupil than programs leading to careers in agriculture, engineering, nursing, or business.

What to Do? A New Vision

This is hardly the first time that Americans have been concerned about how to find enough quality teachers. The largely feminine work force has always been characterized by high turnover and low salaries. Only a generation ago, however, teachers, both male and female, were willing to trade income and advancement opportunities for public esteem, a convenient work schedule, and ideals about public service. When, after the post–World War II baby boom, we had a severe teacher shortage in some fields, the ad hoc incremental solutions to the problem—college scholarships, forgivable loans, and summer institutes— helped a great deal. So did draft deferment for male teachers. But such fundamental changes have overtaken the labor market for females and minorities since the 1960s that an overhaul of the whole personnel system and a rethinking of the teaching profession is necessary now.

The teachers themselves have been rethinking their profession in a very practical way. Between 1965 and 1975 teachers' unions spread rapidly through 35 states. They are now commonplace everywhere except the Southeast. While only 18 percent of the total California work force is unionized, over 90 percent of California's teachers belong to a union. In my view, the rapid spread of unions was a defensive reaction to the deteriorating situation teachers faced with respect to public esteem, pay, and working conditions. A recent poll (on the facing page) further reveals why some teachers feel they must organize to help themselves: Teachers and the public are far apart in their views of problems facing the schools.

Unionization and collective bargaining are subtly altering social relations in the schools as well as conceptions of teaching as an occupation.[5] Clearly, strikes and "work-to-the-rule" slowdowns have soured relationships among teachers, between teachers and administrators, and between teachers and school board members. But relatively few communities have suffered genuinely bitter strikes. More significantly, reliance on the contract as an instrument of job definition has tilted teaching away from its identification as a craft or profession and given it a working-class orientation. Teaching thus becomes a service-sector job like many others. But unionization also has its benefits, such as improved teacher morale, increased per-pupil expenditures, and local responsiveness to federal mandates for equitable treatment of women and minorities. In all union effects, there are large variations among schools, even schools within the same district, depending in large part on the relationship between the principal and the teachers.

Teachers' unions have resisted differential pay for subject areas like physics and math, which are currently experiencing severe shortages. Private universities like Stanford pay medical, law, and business professors more than teachers of the humanities because of market con-

Teachers and Public Have Different Views of
Problems Facing the Schools [6]

Public school teachers rank parents' lack of interest as the most serious problem in schools—a view shared by few Americans—according to a recent Gallup Poll.

The survey, sponsored by Phi Delta Kappa, an educators' fraternity, found 31 percent of teachers cited parents' lack of interest as the top educational problem. Only 5 percent of the general public agreed with that perception.

Other problems named by teachers included inadequate funding of schools (21 percent), students' lack of interest and truancy (20 percent), and lack of discipline (19 percent).

The general public often expressed different concerns. A 27 percent plurality of adults ranked discipline as the top school problem, followed by drug use (18 percent) and poor curriculum and poor standards (15 percent).

The public was much more likely than teachers to see schools as ridden with lax discipline and widespread drug use. One in 3 adults said discipline was a very serious school problem—twice the ratio of teachers who thought so.

A 53 percent majority of the public—but just 17 percent of teachers—said that drug use occurs "most of the time" or "fairly often" at school.

Consistent with these concerns, the public rated schools more negatively than teachers did. Nearly 2 in 3 teachers gave their schools grades of A or B, compared to 4 in 10 adults.

Other differences of opinion between the general public and teachers:
• The public favored the concept of merit pay for teachers, 76 to 19 percent, while teachers were opposed, 64 to 32 percent.
• The public favored requiring students to pass standardized tests for grade promotion, 71 to 25 percent. Teachers rejected the idea, 52 to 43 percent.
• The public supported a national test for high school graduates, 65 to 29 percent. Teachers were much more skeptical, with 48 percent in favor and 45 percent opposed.

Both teachers and the public backed voluntary school prayer, but teachers did so by 2 to 1, while the public supported voluntary prayer by 4 to 1.

Findings were based on a mail survey of 813 elementary and secondary school teachers, selected at random from a list compiled by Market Data Retrieval of Westport, Conn. The margin of sampling error was 4 percentage points. Figures for the general public were from personal interviews with 1,515 adults. That survey's margin of error was 3 points.

——*National Washington Post Weekly* (October 8, 1984)

During the 1950s, teachers began to form unions, to engage in collective bargaining, and to strike. Between 1955 and 1967–68 the number of strikes in a single year rose from 35 to 114.

ditions. But elementary and secondary school unions block this adjustment and advocate across-the-board increases for all teachers. Several states have circumvented the union's position by earmarking summer school classes for teachers in areas of short supply. Some businesses will employ secondary school physics and math teachers for the summer. The idea is to provide 12-month rather than nine-and-one-half-month guaranteed employment for teachers in subjects where there are severe shortages.

Teachers' unions have not resisted computer-assisted instruction, although they might have done so on the basis that automation could cost some teachers jobs. Thus far, personal computers and television have been assigned as supplements to the personal contact between teachers and children. Indeed, many teachers hope that computers can provide children with routine drill and memory exercises, while they focus on complex thinking skills. If future computer systems were designed to replace teachers, the unions would probably mount

Rules for Teachers (1915) in Westwood,* California[7]

1. Not to get married.
2. Not to keep company with men.
3. To be home between the hours of 8 P.M. and 6 A.M. unless in the attendance of a school function.
4. Not to loiter in ice cream stores.
5. Not to leave town at any time without permission of the chairman of the school board.
6. Not to smoke cigarettes.
7. Not to get in a carriage or automobile with any man, except her father or brother.
8. Not to dress in bright colors.
9. Not to dye her hair.
10. To wear at least two petticoats.
11. Not to wear dresses more than two inches above the ankle.
12. To keep the schoolroom neat and clean: Scrub the floor at least once weekly with hot water and soap; sweep the floor at least once daily; clean blackboards at least once daily; start the fire at 7 A.M. so the room will be warm by 8 A.M.

*Now part of Los Angeles Unified School District.

more resistance. But instructional computer software is still in such an embryonic state that there is no immediate danger of a teacher-free computer curriculum.

The unions, however, have not been able to revamp the professional structure and image of teaching. Only this major step will overcome the numerous historical and systemic negative forces that drain the existing teaching force of numbers and quality. Treating one component at a time—beginning salaries, for instance, or education courses at universities—will not be enough. A number of interlocking conditions must be improved simultaneously. A consensus to work for change must be built, one that includes classroom teachers, professors of education, the broader academic community, and the appropriate state and local officials.

As I have emphasized, in status, salaries, and paths for advancement, teaching does not exemplify the characteristics of a profession, at least as the medical or legal professions define that term. For a majority of entrants, teaching is a short career, lasting only five to seven years. Unlike lawyers or doctors, teachers do not control entry

Teacher in an open-style classroom giving a lesson in reading and in manners at the same time.

to their profession. Instead, entry is legislated by the state, and every time a teacher shortage occurs, states waive their minimum entry requirements. For example, the National Science Teachers Association reports that in 1981 over half of the newly employed science and math teachers in secondary schools were employed on an emergency basis because no qualified teachers could be found.

The theoretical and practical knowledge base of teaching is alleged to be small—teaching is an art as well as a science. Pedagogy courses are not held in high public or academic esteem for the special knowledge they convey. The preparation program for many teachers ends at the undergraduate level or with a one-year master's degree program at most, compared to three years for law, six years for medicine, and so on. There is no career ladder for advancement beyond a probationary period of one to three years. Teachers have little control over the flow of their work. In fact, they have a very short time to prepare for their classes because they are assigned to teach throughout their workday. Or, if they are not in the classroom, they are occupied with a broad array of assigned activities, none of which is professional in nature (hall patrol, cafeteria duty, and so on). Often, teachers set for themselves an agenda of non-professional activities; that is, many moonlight in other jobs to supplement their low pay. Finally, as I have stressed throughout, teachers are held responsible by the public for such a broad array of outcomes that the typical elementary school teacher has an unclear idea of her or his professional duty.

Theodore Sizer of Harvard eloquently expresses the situation of many public secondary school teachers:

> Most jobs in the real world have a gap between what would be nice and what is possible. One adjusts. The tragedy for many high school teachers is that the gap is a chasm, not crossed by reasonable and judicious adjustments. Even after adroit accommodations and devastating compromise—only *five minutes per week* of attention on the written work of each student and an average of ten minutes of planning for each fifty-odd-minute class—the task is already crushing, in reality a sixty-hour work week. For this, Horace is paid a wage enjoyed by age-mates in semiskilled and low-pressure blue-collar jobs and by novices, twenty-five years his junior, in some other white-collar professions. Furthermore, none of these sixty-plus hours is spent in replenishing his academic capital . . . [T]here is no pay for upgrading his teachers' skills. [8]

To solve all these deeply rooted problems will be no easy task. Most teaching takes place behind a classroom door; there is little exchange among teachers. Teachers report little variety to teaching work over the years, and they experience few rewards. As Gary Sykes observes, "Autonomy behind the classroom door is won at the price of collegiality and the opportunity to participate in schoolwide educational decision making."[9] Collegiality, evaluation of teachers by other teachers, and rewards for innovation are rare. We must remake the culture of the schools as well as rethink the essence of professionalism in teaching.

What are some of the specific steps to overcome the causes of lagging professionalism? Where should we begin to make fundamental alterations in the assumptions about teaching? Because the problems of the profession are interlocking, the suggestions that follow are listed in no particular order of priority. All are essential steps.

• If the profession is to convince the public that the teacher is a trained professional, it must upgrade its standards for entry. Currently, in several states, students graduating from teachers' training programs are given a basic-skills test, an examination that tests college graduates at a level of difficulty appropriate to college freshmen. Such a test should be administered as a condition for entry to teachers' education, rather than for exit, as is now the case in California. At the point of graduation from a training program, prospective teachers should take an examination analogous to the bar exam for lawyers, followed by a carefully supervised internship.

• Career ladders must be institutionalized to increase the professional responsibilities of experienced teachers. A ladder might include career steps such as master or mentor teacher; a teacher at this higher level would develop new curricula and help novices. Such teachers should be paid about the same as middle managers in business.

• Teachers should play a larger role in selection, evaluation, and in-service development within their own ranks. They should disavow no-fault teaching, establish their own standards for good practice, and establish peer review to recommend promotion or to judge incompetence.

• Universities should form partnerships with teachers in order to develop teaching methods that can be validated and then used to prepare beginning teachers.

• Teachers should become more involved at the school building or school site level in finding solutions for educational problems. Teachers' committees at each school site could work cooperatively on curriculum policy, student assessment, and school improvement. In Chapter 7, I outlined a specific plan for returning control from central authorities to the school site. This plan would improve teachers' morale as well as bring control closer to the parents.

• States and local districts should clarify disciplinary policies so that teachers have clear authority in the classroom.

• Pay should be increased, working conditions improved, and teaching loads reduced in some subjects, such as writing. No writing teacher can handle 150 to 200 students effectively each day if he or she is to correct individual writing assignments. The American public must be ready to pay more taxes for better teachers. Career ladder plans like Tennessee's, if implemented across the nation, would cost about $7.5 billion nationally.

• The school boards and state officials must agree on a framework for a curriculum that teachers can realistically cover. We cannot expect the typical elementary teacher to teach reading, writing, several varieties of arithmetic, geography, spelling, science, economics, music, art, and history—and at the same time help children to develop physically, morally, and individually, and strive to mold them into good citizens.

States such as California and Florida are holding out a variety of lures for attracting and retaining better teachers. What will be the cost-effectiveness of loan forgiveness, scholarships, merit pay, a higher minimum salary, and mentor teaching positions? Which of these concepts will retain the most teachers? We are clearly at the experimental stage—or "the cutting edge of ignorance"—about what types and amounts of incentives most attract prospective and current teachers.

CHAPTER

LOOKING
AHEAD

As parents, most Americans want their children "to have it all."
As taxpayers, however, they are apt to act as though they prefer
an educational system focused on the three R's. To stabilize this im-
balance, we must face and answer the question: How much can and
should the schools contribute to that broad and necessary education
that prepares Americans to cope, to work, and to use their free time
in rewarding pursuits? I do not agree with those who suggest that
the schools should confine themselves to a narrow program of
"basics," that they should, for example, abandon art and music.
Rather, we must assign to the schools what they can do best and
surrender other functions to more specialized agencies outside the
school system.

Coalition Building

Who might become part of a political coalition to reformulate the
objectives for public education in a tough-minded and coherent way?
Members of the education profession itself must be major participants;
administrators must be willing to prune their bureaucracies and hum-
ble their empires. Some steps in this direction have already been taken.
After the passage of Proposition 13 in California in 1978, for example,
many local schools eliminated adult education divisions, dispersing
their activities among the community colleges. Similarly, the secondary
schools should surrender most of their programs in health, the worthy
use of leisure, driver's training, and vocational skills. Most comprehensive secondary schools should leave the development of highly
technical and specific job skills to postsecondary or other regional

public or private schools. These institutions can afford to buy new equipment frequently and can use part-time teachers from industry to keep pace with rapid changes in the workplace.

If these difficult reallocations are to succeed, the professional educators must be supported by allies such as the PTA, business groups, organized labor, and other powerful lobbies. Other public agencies and private institutions must be willing (or pressured) to take over the functions that schools spin off. Public health, recreation, and child care units of the city and county governments must help the schools by providing more children's services. Job-training programs managed by communities or private concerns must be expanded.

Cost-Effective Changes

To create and maintain top-quality schools will not be inexpensive. To attract and retain high-quality teachers, a number of policy changes must be made simultaneously; among them, the raising of salaries is crucial. It would cost about $20 billion to increase the average teacher's salary of $23,000 by $10,000! The public may be willing to raise taxes in order to attract and hold better teachers, but not until they have confidence in the public schools and believe that academic attainment is increasing.

To respect the limitations on public funding means giving careful attention to the relative costs of educational improvements. An evaluation of four different strategies for improvement has revealed significant differences in cost. The four strategies are these: (1) reducing class size by adding more teachers, (2) increasing the length of the school day, (3) using computers to facilitate instruction, and (4) providing tutors—peer or adult. A study measured the gain in pupils' achievement scores in reading and mathematics purchased by $300 in funding for each approach. In general, peer tutoring proved the most cost-effective, and reducing class size and increasing the length of the school day the least cost-effective. Computer-assisted instruction ranked between these extremes.[1] Other studies have demonstrated that large achievement gains can be brought about by homework, if it is carefully graded. Teachers must have the time, however, to do the necessary grading.

Evaluation is essential: Many recently adopted state policies devote large sums of money to the approach with the lowest potential for gain—lengthening the school day or year. Extending the school day by 20 percent (from 6.5 hours to 8 hours) would cost more than $20

Back to basics?

billion; lengthening the school year by 20 percent (from 180 days to 220 days) would also cost $20 billion.[2] Expensive reforms of this kind are a gamble: More time spent in school may not mean more time spent in learning. The key is what educators do with more time. Schools could lengthen the learning day simply by using the valuable school time wasted now, for example, when teachers have students do homework in class or spend 20 percent of class time establishing order and organizing instructional tasks.

A national study revealed that within a school day of equal length, some schools spend nearly half again as much time on instruction as others do.[3] Many studies demonstrate that an increase in academic instructional time *if used appropriately* will lead to higher achievement in the academic area covered. As a first step, high schools should increase time on instructional tasks in academic areas, particularly writing, math, and science. Although the time devoted to a task is only one of many variables that make up good schooling, it is a variable more easily changed than some others—retraining thousands of teachers, for instance.

Frequent classroom interruptions—announcements on loudspeakers, students entering and leaving for special activities—waste crucial learning time. The Texas legislature has taken stern measures to ensure that their schools give top priority to academic achievement. One of the new policies being enforced mandates automatic failure for any student who has more than five unexcused absences a semester. Unexcused absences include such things as band performances and golf tournaments.

Curricular Reform

Colleges can encourage and reinforce improvements in secondary education simply by requiring more academic courses for admission and by giving increased weight to higher level academic courses. The California state university and college system, for example, admits students on the basis of grade averages. Every course is given the same weight except for physical education; a grade of B in photography counts for as much as a B in physics. Leaders of higher education are reluctant to call for a drastic tightening-up of standards, because an 18 percent drop in the number of 18-year-olds is expected during the 1980s. University trustees must adopt priorities higher than the mere sustaining of all existing faculty members and the courses they offer.

A new conception of the high school core curriculum—or of a general education—must precede any raising of academic standards. Although such a change does not require large sums of money, it calls for other valuable assets—will and imagination. Most past reforms with a lasting impact have added new organizational layers and functions to high schools, such as the vocational and driver's education courses we have discussed. But the limited fiscal resources projected for the 1980s imply the need for concentration on the very reforms that have *not* left a residue—changes in classroom techniques and content within the core academic areas. As Gordon Cawelti writes:

> It seems increasingly clear that there needs to be some synthesizing of the patchwork curriculum into a more coherent pattern of learning experiences which focus on *both* individual needs and those of society. This suggests more interdisciplinary courses out of which advanced elective courses must continue. Since schools clearly do not have the

time for all to have individual courses in art, music, theater, literature, and the like, a unified humanities course showing the interrelationship of all these subjects is more feasible.[4]

Although it is imperative that the high school curriculum retain an offering of elective courses that will capitalize on student interests, these must evolve from a core of general studies. Schools have been pressured into developing instructional courses in drug abuse, sex education, moral education, energy, career education, ethnic studies, parenting, environment, and so on. Rarely do educators or the public ask what is to be excluded when these new curricular foci are introduced, or where they should be placed in the total pattern of instruction. Educational reform in the 1980s should not simply add new layers and functions to existing ones. What is needed is a balancing of functions, a realism in claims, and a focus on a core curriculum that schools can implement. The California State Board of Education, for example, will now request all school districts to review the high school courses offered in the light of enrollment, the quality of instructional materials, and attempts to provide coherent sequences in science and literature. Educators should also strive to make required courses more interesting as well as more difficult. The recent reports have neglected the importance of student motivation.

Another way to focus the goals of our high schools is to capitalize on the success of big-city "magnet high schools." Each of these magnet schools has a particular academic theme, such as performing arts, public service, health professions, humanities/communications, or science/engineering. In Dallas, Texas, for example, a student daily spends a block of three hours on the special curriculum. The rest of the school day is devoted to instruction at either the magnet site or the student's home school. Students from anywhere in Dallas can attend one of the magnet schools if they have a special interest in its themes. Ethnic balance is considered, but admission is on a first-come-first-served basis. There are no academic entrance screens. Such magnet or theme high schools can provide up-to-date vocational education by aggregating modern equipment and specialized teachers—elements usually too scarce to be spread out over each comprehensive high school.

In Dallas, these magnet schools have assisted in desegregation and on tests have registered the most rapid student academic growth. A theme approach to the high school curriculum provides more choices for students, decentralized decision making at the school sites, and instruction for all students in those academic skills emphasized by the central district office. It is this balance—a balance of central curricular standards (or a core curriculum) and depth within particular subject areas—that was missing in so many secondary school transcripts that I examined during my years on the state board of education.

Political Strategies

I am cautiously optimistic that steps taken in 1983 and 1984 to raise academic standards will increase high school achievement. A national trend toward higher scores on standardized tests—if it develops— would strengthen public confidence and could even galvanize political support for increased funding for education. Without an increase in funding, however, greater academic emphasis can only take dollars away from the special programs for the disadvantaged and handicapped. The threatening, competitive social and economic context of the eighties requires sophisticated political understanding and insight on the part of leaders in education. Educators and their supporting organizations will have to continue to work through the traditional political processes of lobbying and elections. With state financing of public schools a growing trend, and large-scale federal increases in funding unlikely, political activists will have to focus on state government, making campaign contributions and carrying on campaign work for state political candidates. In Florida, where the largest portion of the population consists of retirees who contend that they have already paid once for education in some other state, local educators have reluctantly supported de facto full state assumption of school finance. The future in many states may look very much like this.

Education often consumes between 40 and 70 percent of a state budget. Funding for schools in states that have direct voting on such issues will therefore be vulnerable to initiatives that place limitations on spending. Organizations of teachers should redirect to state political campaigns and lobbying much of the effort now expended at the national level. In many states the political split between parents and teachers needs to be bridged. Educators should target special campaign efforts for specific friends or enemies. The political strategies outlined here may seem too partisan, but the political situation is far from ideal.[5]

Should education leaders engage in internecine warfare and fail to form coalitions, the rate of increase in expenditures for schools will be much lower than in the period from 1970 to 1980. As the trend away from reliance on the local property tax as a source of financing the public schools continues, supporters of public education will have to play a more aggressive role in state politics. There is a danger that militant political action during a time of retrenchment will further decrease public confidence in education. A backlash could arise against education as merely another special interest using its political muscle to serve narrow self-interest. Militancy will not attract a broad base of followers in the absence of renewal of loyalty to public education as a public good, essential for civic learning and the instilling of democratic values.

Control of the Schools

There has been an enormous growth in the degree of control that courts, federal and state government, and private testing agencies exercise over our schools. Some of this growth has been good. But the steady and unremitting loss of local control of education is cause for concern. The local school board is increasingly a convenient flak-catcher with little authority or discretion to ameliorate causes of citizens' complaints. We need to restore more control to local authorities, while we retain central development and management of policies in the national and state interest—eliminating racial and gender bias or setting minimum academic standards.

Reforms in school governance, however, should be approached with caution. A major theme of this volume is the complexity of the present system of governance. Not surprisingly, no accepted theory allows us to predict what changes will result from specific reforms in school governance, such as those outlined in Chapter 7. Federal and state categorical programs have assumed that predictable changes would result from regulations and earmarked money, but these expectations were often not realized. Such experiences suggest that changes in governance should take place gradually, accompanied by careful evaluation at each stage.

If the schools had fewer and more attainable objectives, then the recurrent cycles of "reform" would be moderated—cycles like the current one in which advocates of traditional education and "excellence" have replaced supporters of equity as the most forceful constituency. The bandwagons would not roll as often, and continuity, built upon

Looking ahead.

limited purposes, would develop. Although the cycles reflect societal conditions, they are also caused in large part by entrenched expectations and by the schools' inability to satisfy the many constituencies these reflect.

Most importantly, then, the public, which ultimately controls education policy, needs to help the schools by realizing that public education cannot "do it all." We may all wish the schools could satisfy every objective listed in Chapter 4, but we must realize that they do not have the resources to accomplish these goals simultaneously. Limiting our expectations for our schools will not be politically easy. Parents will have to assume responsibilities that they have been happy to unload upon the schools. It requires leaders who will dramatize the lack of realism in public expectations and unite a coalition around a new consensus on the highest priorities for the common school.

Setting priorities is essentially a struggle for control, and there will never be an end to the struggle for control of America's public schools.

The values and philosophies of the contestants are deeply rooted and conflicting. An approach we have used since the 1920s to resolve this conflict is to make our schools provide something for everybody. No one is to be disappointed. In governance, the approach of giving everyone a voice in running the schools has often fragmented power to the point where everyone and no one seems in charge. The schools have been giving Americans what they want, but few people are satisfied and many are disappointed.

A promising turning point toward rethinking our school goals and governance, however, seems to have been reached in the past two years. My preliminary surveys indicate that academic standards are increasing and becoming more precise. High school pupils in California, for example, are taking more academic subjects, and their transcripts reveal more coherence in course selection. The Gallup Poll in fall 1984 registered an encouraging jump in public confidence in the public schools. But it is the people in our democracy who will decide whether the 1983-85 movement toward academic excellence is enduring or just another swing of the pendulum. Will we go too far and create excessive state control of local schools? Will we create an overly narrow curriculum? Will we set too narrow a range of goals for a student body of increasing ethnic diversity? Or will we this time strike a balance that lasts?

NOTES

Chapter 2

Among the 1983 reports on education are:

Mortimer J. Adler, *The Paideia Proposal* (New York: Macmillan, 1982).

Ernest L. Boyer, *High School* (New York: Harper and Row, 1983).

College Board Educational Equality Project, *Academic Preparation for College: What Students Need to Know and Be Able to Do* (New York: College Board, 1983).

Education Commission of the States' Task Force on Education for Economic Growth, *Action for Excellence* (Denver: Education Commission of the States, 1983).

John I. Goodlad, *A Place Called School: Prospects for the Future* (New York: McGraw-Hill, 1984).

National Commission on Excellence in Education, *A Nation at Risk* (Washington, D.C.: U.S. Government Printing Office, 1983).

National Science Board Commission on Precollege Education in Mathematics, Science, and Technology, *Educating Americans for the 21st Century* (Washington, D.C.: U.S. Government Printing Office, 1983).

Theodore R. Sizer, *Horace's Compromise: The Dilemma of the American High School* (Boston: Houghton Mifflin, 1984).

Twentieth Century Fund Task Force on Federal Elementary and Secondary Education Policy, *Making the Grade* (New York: Twentieth Century Fund, 1983).

Critiques of the reports can be found in the following articles:

Harold Howe II, "Education Moves to Center Stage: An Overview of Recent Studies," *Phi Delta Kappan* (November 1983).

Thomas James and David Tyack, "Learning from Past Efforts to Reform the High School," *Phi Delta Kappan*, (February 1983).

For another perspective on the current state of public education see:

Michael W. Kirst and Walter I. Garms, "The Political Environment of School Finance Policy in the 1980s," in James Guthrie, ed., *School Finance Policy and Practices* (Cambridge: Ballinger, 1980).

[1] Paul E. Peterson, "Did the Education Commissions Say Anything?" *Brookings Review*, vol. 2 (1983): 4.

[2] *USA Today*, July 27, 1984.
[3] Henry Levin, *Education Vouchers and Social Policy*, Stanford University: Institute for Research on Educational Finance and Governance, Project Report (1979) 17.

Chapter 3

[1] David B. Tyack and Elisabeth Hansot, *Managers of Virtue* (New York: Basic Books, 1982) 94.
[2] David B. Tyack, "Needed: The Reform of a Reform," in William E. Dickerson, ed., *New Dimensions in School Board Leadership* (1969): 30-31.
[3] David B. Tyack, *The One Best System: A History of American Urban Education* (Cambridge: Harvard University Press, 1974).
[4] Samuel P. Hays, "The Politics of Reform in Municipal Government in the Progressive Era," *Pacific Northwest Quarterly* 55 (1963): 163.
[5] George S. Counts, *The Social Composition of Boards of Education* (Chicago: University of Chicago Press, 1927).
[6] See Tyack and Hansot, *Managers of Virtue*, 138–139.
[7] David B. Tyack, Robert Lowe, and Elisabeth Hansot, *Public Schools in Hard Times* (Cambridge: Harvard University Press) 144-152, 189-196.
[8] Clarence Karier, "Education of the American Citizen: An Historical Critique." Unpublished paper (Champaign-Urbana: University of Illinois, 1978).

Chapter 4

[1] Ronald Gross and Paul Osterman, *High School* (New York: Simon and Schuster, 1971) 31.
[2] David B. Tyack, "The High School as a Social Service Agency: Historical Perspectives on Current Policy Issues," in *Educational Evaluation and Policy Analysis* (September-October 1979): 45-46.
[3] James Koerner, *Who Controls American Education?* (Boston: Beacon Press, 1968) 126-127.
[4] Launor F. Carter, "The Sustaining Effects Study of Compensatory and Elementary Education," *Educational Researcher* (August–September 1984): 4–7.

Chapter 5

[1] Horace Mann, *Twelfth Annual Report of the Secretary of the Board of Education, West Newton, Massachusetts, November 24, 1848* (Boston: Dutton, Wentworth State Printers, 1849).
[2] Torsten Husén, "Are Standards in U.S. Schools Really Lagging Behind Those in Other Countries?" *Phi Delta Kappan* (March 1983): 458.
[3] Perry Garfinkel, "The Best 'Jewish Mother' in the World," *Psychology Today* (September 1983): 56.

Chapter 7

[1,2] Copyright © 1969, 1971 by American Heritage Publishing Co., Inc. Reprinted by permission of Harper and Row Publishers, Inc.
[3] Theodore Sizer, *Horace's Compromise: The Dilemma of the American High School* (Boston: Houghton Mifflin, 1984) 217.

Chapter 8

1. For details on all these matters, see W. Timothy Weaver, *America's Teacher Quality Problem* (New York: Praeger, 1983).
2. Gary Sykes, "Contradictions, Ironies, and Promises Unfulfilled: A Contemporary Account of the Status of Teaching," *Phi Delta Kappan* (October 1983): 87-93.
3. Sykes, "Contradictions," 92.
4. Donna Kerr, "Teaching Competence and Teacher Education in the United States," in Lee Shulman and Gary Sykes, eds., *Handbook of Teaching and Policy* (New York: Longman, 1983) 135-36.
5. Sykes, "Contradictions," 87-93.
6. "Teachers Say Parents' Lack of Interest Is Biggest Problem," *National Washington Post Weekly* (October 8, 1984): 38.
7. From the collection of David B. Tyack, Stanford University.
8. Theodore Sizer, *Horace's Compromise*, 20. See also J. Myron Atkin, "Who Will Teach in High School?" *Daedalus* (Summer 1981): 91–104.
9. Sykes, "Contradictions," 93.

Chapter 9

1. Henry Levin, Gene Glass, and Gail Meister, *Cost-Effectiveness of Four Educational Interventions.* Stanford University: Institute for Research on Educational Finance and Governance, Project Report (1984).
2. Allan Odden, "Financing Excellence," *Phi Delta Kappan* (January 1984).
3. Goodlad, *A Place Called School*, 97–100.
4. Gordon Cawelti, "Redesigning General Education in American High Schools," paper presented at the Annual Convention of the National Association of Secondary School Principals, Miami, Florida, 1980.
5. For an expansion of this argument see Michael W. Kirst, "Loss of Support for Public Secondary Schools: Some Causes and Solutions," *Daedalus* (Summer 1981): 45-68.

SUGGESTIONS
FOR FURTHER
READING

Cremin, Lawrence. *The Transformation of the School*. New York: Vintage Books, 1964.

Garms, Walter, James Guthrie, and Lawrence Pierce. *School Finance*. Englewood Cliffs, NJ: Prentice-Hall, 1979.

Goodlad, John I. *A Place Called School: Prospects for the Future*. New York: McGraw-Hill, 1984.

Husén, Torsten. *The School in Question*. New York: Oxford University Press, 1979.

Ravitch, Diane. *The Troubled Crusade: American Education, 1945–1980*. New York: Basic Books, 1983.

Rohlen, Thomas P. *Japan's High Schools*. Berkeley: University of California Press, 1983.

Sizer, Theodore. *Horace's Compromise: The Dilemma of the American High School*. Boston: Houghton Mifflin, 1983.

Tyack, David B. *The One Best System: A History of American Urban Education*. Cambridge: Harvard University Press, 1974.

Tyack, David B., Robert Lowe, and Elisabeth Hansot. *Public Schools in Hard Times: The Great Depression and Recent Years*. Cambridge: Harvard University Press, 1984.

ABOUT
THE AUTHOR

Michael Kirst's breadth of expertise is reflected in the various appointments he holds at Stanford University: Professor of Education, School of Education; Professor (by courtesy), Graduate School of Business; Affiliated Professor, Department of Political Science.

After earning his Master of Public Administration and then his Ph.D. at Harvard in 1964, Professor Kirst began a career in Washington, D.C., that was to combine administration, finance, and education. He served first as Budget Examiner, U.S. Bureau of the Budget, then worked in education planning for the U.S. Office of Education. His final assignment, before coming to Stanford in 1969, was as Staff Director, U.S. Senate Subcommittee on Manpower, Employment and Poverty. Appointed to the California State Board of Education in 1975, he served as board president from 1977 to 1981.

Professor Kirst has traveled widely as consultant to and observer of schools across the United States, in Europe, and in the Orient. The range of his interests, which includes school politics, finance, curriculum, and history, is evident in the several books and numerous articles he has published. He has been a vice-president of the American Education Research Association and is a member of the National Academy of Education. His present research includes a study of the changing external context of the U.S. secondary school for the Stanford and the Schools Project.

Mike Kirst knows the public school system not only as a scholar and reformer, but as a parent of two children who are recent graduates of public schools.

PICTURE CREDITS

Cover and book design by Andrew Danish

INDEX

Page references for illustrations, tables, figures, and sidebars are indicated in italics. An "m." indicates a brief mention.

Religion, education and, 24, 27, 28. *See also* Prayer in school

Reform: need for understanding in historical context of, xv–xvi, 18–19; cycles in, 7–21; and multiple constituencies, 7–14; positive achievements of past, 9, 130; and the media, 14–16; overburdening legacies of, 9, 11–14, 49–54; proposals for future, 16–17, 157–65; of common school, 32–39; initiatives in California, 1958–75, 47; current, 58; and 1983 overcorrection, 65–67. *See also* Crises in education; Educational policy; Goals

Reports, national: of 1983, 14, 17–19, 58, 130; listed, 167; predicted for 1990s, 17

Riis, Jacob, *5, 20, 25*

Riles, Wilson, Jr., 95

Riley, Richard, 15

Rote learning, 87

Rural schools, *4, 27, 42, 100,* 102, 103

Russian educational system, 41, 74, 92

Salaries, teachers', *see* Teachers: salaries of

Salt Lake City, Ut., 58

San Antonio v. Rodriguez, 1973, 101

San Francisco earthquake, textbooks compared on, 119–20

San Jose, Calif., 50, 97; m. 132

Schedules, students' typical, *59, 64*

Schlechty, Philip, 141

Scholastic Aptitude Test (SAT), 1, 84, 89–90, *90,* 92, 141

School Board Journal, The, 96, 113

School boards, 3, 31–32, 63–64, 95, 133–35

School day, 67, 77–78, 127, 158–59

School Improvement Program (SIP), 126, 130–35, 154

Schools, overburdened, 3, 9, 11–14, 49–54; solutions for problems of, 5, 157–65; performance of, 73–93; current trends in control of, 125–26, 163–65

School year, 5, 9, *10,* 19, 67, 70, 82, *83,* 158; m. 127

Science, 41, 77, *78,* 81, 87, 91; m. 17, 65

Secondary education, *see* High schools

Segregation, 24, 25; m. 135. *See also* Black students

Selectivity, schools', 52

Self-esteem, schools' duty to encourage, 51

Sendai, Japan, 85, 86

Sex education, m. 161

Sex-stereotyping, 42; m. 24, 47, 121. *See also* Women

Sizer, Theodore R., 135, 153

Smith-Hughes Act of 1918, 35, *35*

Social studies, 44, 54–55, 70, 82

South Carolina, 15

Soviet Union, *see* Russian educational system; Sputnik

Special education programs, *see* Compensatory education; Disadvantaged students; Handicapped students

Special interest groups: expansion of, 12. *See also* Compensatory education; Constituencies, multiple; Disadvantaged students; Handicapped students, Minorities; Vocational education

Sports programs, 64

Sputnik, 7, 8, 17–18, 92, 123; m. 14

Stanford University, 91; m. xvi, 8. 148

State boards of education, 1–2, 3, 112. *See also* California State Board of Education

States: authority of, 24, 95–99, *98,* 102–09; education budget of, 11, 95–109, 162; and local control, 102, 107–09; and egalitarianism, 26, 125–26; and current reforms, 126–29

Stevenson, Harold W., 85, 86

Stockholm, University of, 74

Stress in schooling, 88

Strikes, teacher, 45, 148, *150;* m. 140

Students: enrollment of, 10, 11, *34, 138;* ratio of, to teachers, 1920–50, *37;* attainment of, 73–74; international comparisons of, 73–89; future demographics of, 138

Superintendents: challenged, 11–12, 44; early 20th-century powers of, 32, 33, 38

Supreme Court and segregation, 25, *48,* 101

Sustaining Effects Study, 65, *68*